CONTEMPORARY'S

GED

TEST 4: LITERATURE AND THE ARTS

CONTEMPORARY'S

GED
TEST 4: LITERATURE AND THE ARTS

PREPARATION FOR THE HIGH SCHOOL EQUIVALENCY EXAMINATION

Reviewers
June Entringer, GED Instructor
Albuquerque Technical-Vocational Institute
Albuquerque, New Mexico

Gregory Anderson, GED Instructor
Chicago City Colleges, Wilbur Wright Campus
Chicago, Illinois

CONTEMPORARY BOOKS

a division of NTC/CONTEMPORARY PUBLISHING GROUP
Lincolnwood, Illinois USA

NEWLY REVISED

Library of Congress Cataloging-in-Publication Data

GED test 4: literature and the arts.
          p.   cm.
      ISBN 0-8092-3779-2
          1. Literature—Examinations, questions, etc.   2. Arts—
Examinations, questions, etc.   I. Title.
PN62.R64   1994
700'.76—dc20   93-43846
                                                              CIP

Project Editor
Pat Fiene

Writer
Elizabeth Romanek

Contributing Writers
Noreen Giles
Anne McGravie

ISBN: 0-8092-3779-2

Published by Contemporary Books,
a division of NTC/Contemporary Publishing Group, Inc.,
4255 West Touhy Avenue,
Lincolnwood (Chicago), Illinois 60646-1975 U.S.A.
© 1994 NTC/Contemporary Publishing Group, Inc.

  8 9 0 GB 13 12 11 10 9

Editorial Director
Mark Boone

Editorial
Dawn Barker
Christine Benton
Lisa Black
Lynn McEwan
Sharon Rundo

Editorial Assistant
Maggie McCann

Editorial Production Manager
Norma Underwood

Production Assistant
Thomas D. Scharf

Cover Design
Georgene Sainati

Typography
Terrence Alan Stone

Interior Design
Lucy Lesiak

Cover Illustration
Mark Jasin

Contents

Acknowledgments

Excerpt on page 2 from "The Cultures of Illness." Copyright 1993 *U.S. News & World Report.*

Poem on page 5, *Ballad of the Landlord.* Copyright 1951 by Langston Hughes. Copyright renewed 1979 by George Houston Bass.

Excerpt on page 6 from *West Side Story* by Arthur Laurents and Leonard Bernstein. Copyright 1957 by Leonard Bernstein and Stephen Sondheim. Copyright 1956, 1958 by Arthur Laurents, Leonard Bernstein, Stephen Sondheim and Jerome Robbins. Reprinted by permission of Random House, Inc.

Excerpt on page 7 from "To Be a Nominee" by Stephen Schiff. Reprinted by permission; © 1993 Stephen Schiff. Originally in *The New Yorker.*

Excerpt on page 18 from *Balanchine's Complete Stories of the Great Ballets* by George Balanchine and Francis Mason. Copyright 1954, 1968, 1975, 1977 by Doubleday & Company, Inc.

Excerpt on page 19 from *Blue Collar Journal.* Copyright 1974 by John R. Coleman. Reprinted by permission of the author.

Excerpt on page 20 from "Death of a Maverick Mafioso." Copyright 1972 Time Inc. Reprinted by permission.

Excerpt on pages 22–23 from *Long Lance: An Autobiography of an Indian Chief* by Chief Buffalo Child Long Lance. Copyright 1928 by Cosmopolitan Book Corporation. Copyright 1956 by Holt, Rinehart and Winston. Reprinted by permission of Henry Holt and Company, Inc.

Excerpt on page 26 from *Modern Black Stories.* Copyright 1971 by Barron's Educational Series, Inc., Hauppauge, New York.

Excerpt on page 28 from "Vietnam, Vietnam." Copyright 1985. Reprinted by permission of Pete Hamill.

Excerpt on page 32 from "The Puck Stops Here." Reprinted with permission from *Women's Sports and Fitness* magazine.

Excerpt on page 34 from *Barrio Boy* by Ernesto Galarza, © 1971 by the University of Notre Dame Press. Reprinted by permission of the publisher.

Excerpt on page 35 from *The Road to Wigan Pier* by George Orwell. Reprinted by permission of Harcourt Brace & Company and the estate of the late Sonia Brownell Orwell.

Excerpt on page 42 from "The Most Dangerous Game" by Richard Connell. Copyright 1924 by Richard Connell. Copyright renewed 1952 by Louise Fox Connell. Reprinted by permission of Brandt & Brandt Literary Agents, Inc.

Excerpt on page 44 from "A & P" in *Pigeon Feathers and Other Stories* by John Updike. Copyright 1962. Reprinted by permission of Random House, Inc.

Excerpt on page 46 from "The Five-Forty-Eight." Copyright 1978 by John Cheever; reprinted with the permission of Wylie, Aitken & Stone, Inc.

Excerpt on page 47 from "Two Kinds" in *The Joy Luck Club* by Amy Tan. Copyright 1989 by Amy Tan. Reprinted by permission of The Putnam Publishing Group.

Excerpt on page 50 from *A Sense of Where You Are* by John McPhee. Copyright 1965, 1978 by John McPhee. Reprinted by permission of Farrar, Straus & Giroux, Inc.

Excerpt on page 99 from "Shoot the Moon" by Susan Orlean. Reprinted by permission; © 1993 Susan Orlean. Originally in *The New Yorker*.

Excerpt on pages 100–101 from "What Value Are Video Games?" by William B. White, Jr. Reprinted from *USA Today Magazine*, copyright 1992 by the Society for the Advancement of Education.

Excerpt on pages 102–103 from "Soap Operas: A Healthy Habit After All?" by Laura Flynn McCarthy. Courtesy *Vogue* magazine. Copyright 1985 by The Conde Nast Publications Inc.

Excerpt on page 110 first published in *The Reporter*, 26 January 1967. Reprinted from *The Way to Rainy Mountain* by N. Scott Momaday, © 1969 The University of New Mexico Press.

Excerpt on page 111 from "Portraits of a Cop." Reprinted by permission of *Best of The Wall Street Journal*, © 1973 Dow Jones & Company, Inc. All rights reserved worldwide.

Excerpt on page 114 from *The Autobiography of Malcolm X* by Malcolm X with Alex Haley. Copyright 1964 by Alex Haley and Malcolm X. Copyright 1965 by Alex Haley and Betty Shabazz. Reprinted by permission of Random House, Inc.

Excerpt on page 122 from "The Rocking-Horse Winner" by D. H. Lawrence, copyright 1933 by the Estate of D. H. Lawrence, renewed © 1961 by Angelo Ravagli and C. M. Weekley, Executors of the Estate of Frieda Lawrence, from *Complete Short Stories of D. H. Lawrence* by D. H. Lawrence. Used by permission of Viking Penguin, a division of Penguin Books USA Inc.

Excerpt on page 123 from *One Day in the Life of Ivan Denisovich* by Alexander Solzhenitsyn. Copyright 1963 by Frederick A. Praeger, Inc. Reprinted by permission of Henry Holt and Co., Inc.

Excerpt on page 124 from *Light in August* by William Faulkner. Copyright 1932 and renewed 1960 by William Faulkner. Reprinted by permission of Random House, Inc.

Excerpt on page 126 from *Native Son* by Richard Wright. Copyright 1940 by Richard Wright. Copyright renewed 1968 by Ellen Wright. Reprinted by permission of HarperCollins Publishers, Inc.

Excerpt on page 132 from "The Boarding House" in *Dubliners* by James Joyce. Copyright 1916 by B. W. Heubsch. Definitive text © 1967 by the Estate of James Joyce. Used by permission of Viking Penguin, a division of Penguin Books USA Inc.

Excerpt on page 133 from "The Prison" in *The Magic Barrel* by Bernard Malamud. Copyright 1950, 1958 and copyright renewed 1986 by Bernard Malamud. Reprinted by permission of Farrar, Straus & Giroux, Inc.

Excerpt on page 134 from "I Stand Here Ironing," in *Tell Me a Riddle* by Tillie Olsen. Copyright 1956, 1957, 1960, 1961 by Tillie Olsen. Used by permission of Delacorte Press/Seymour Lawrence, a division of Bantam Doubleday Dell Publishing Group, Inc.

Excerpt on page 135 from *The Great Gatsby* (authorized text) by F. Scott Fitzgerald. Copyright 1925 by Charles Scribner's Sons; renewal copyright 1953 by Frances Scott Fitzgerald Lanahan. Copyright 1991, 1992 Eleanor Lanahan, Matthew J. Bruccoli and Samuel J. Lanahan as Trustees under Agreement dated July 3, 1975. Created by Frances Scott Fitzgerald Smith. Reprinted with permission of Charles Scribner's Sons, an imprint of Macmillan Publishing Company.

Excerpt on pages 138–139 from "Sonny's Blues," © 1957 by James Baldwin, from *Going to Meet the Man* by James Baldwin. Used by permission of Doubleday, a division of Bantam Doubleday Dell Publishing Group, Inc.

Poem on page 186, "As You Leave Me" by Etheridge Knight. Permission granted by Broadside Press.

Poem on page 187, "Hay for the Horses," in *Riprap and Cold Mountain Poems* by Gary Snyder. Copyright 1958, 1959, 1965 by Gary Snyder. Reprinted by permission of North Point Press, a division of Farrar, Straus & Giroux, Inc.

Excerpt on page 189 from "Ex-Basketball Player" in *The Carpentered Hen and Other Tame Creatures* by John Updike. Copyright 1957, 1982 by John Updike. Reprinted by permission of Alfred A. Knopf, Inc.

Poem on page 192, "Daybreak," © 1977 by Gary Soto. Reprinted from *The Elements of San Joaquin*, by Gary Soto, by permission of the University of Pittsburgh Press.

Excerpts on pages 196–197 from *Of Mice and Men* by John Steinbeck. Copyright 1937, renewed 1965 by John Steinbeck. Used by permission of Viking Penguin, a division of Penguin Books USA Inc.

Excerpt on page 205 from *The Odd Couple* by Neil Simon. Copyright 1986 by Neil Simon. Reprinted by permission of Random House, Inc.

Excerpt on pages 207–208 from *Fences* by August Wilson. Copyright 1986 by August Wilson. Used by permission of New American Library, a division of Penguin Books USA Inc.

Excerpt on pages 210–211 from *A Doll's House* in *The Complete Major Prose Plays of Henrik Ibsen* by Henrik Ibsen, translated by Rolf Fjelde. Translation © 1965, 1970, 1978 by Rolf Fjelde. Used by permission of New American Library, a division of Penguin Books USA Inc.

Excerpt on pages 214–220 from *Death of a Salesman* by Arthur Miller. Copyright 1949, renewed 1977 by Arthur Miller. Used by permission of Viking Penguin, a division of Penguin Books USA Inc.

Excerpt on page 222 from *Fool for Love*, © 1983 by Sam Shepard in *Fool for Love and Other Plays* by Sam Shepard. Used by permission of Bantam Books, a division of Bantam Doubleday Dell Publishing Group, Inc.

Excerpt on page 224 from *Cat on a Hot Tin Roof* by Tennessee Williams. Copyright 1954, 1955, 1971 by Tennessee Williams. Reprinted by permission of New Directions Publishing Corporation.

Excerpt on page 226 from *A Raisin in the Sun* by Lorraine Hansberry. Copyright 1958 by Robert Nemiroff as an unpublished work. Copyright 1959, 1966, 1984 by Robert Nemiroff. Copyright renewed 1987 by Robert Nemiroff. Reprinted by permission of Random House, Inc.

Excerpt on page 238 from "The Harlem Unit" from *Black Theater in America* by James Haskins (Thomas Y. Crowell, 1982). Reprinted by permission of author.

Excerpt on pages 240–241 from *The Great Television Heroes* by Donald Glut and Jim Harmon. Copyright 1975. Reprinted by permission of Doubleday, a division of Bantam Doubleday Dell Publishing Group, Inc.

Excerpt on page 242 from Video Yesteryear catalog. All descriptions and entire contents © 1991 Video Yesteryear. All rights reserved.

Excerpt on page 244 from *Singers and Sweethearts: The Women of Country Music*. Copyright 1977 Silver Eagle Publishers, Inc. Reprinted by permission.

Excerpt on page 246 from "Star of 'Tap Dance Kid' Started Living Title Role More Than Half a Century Ago" by Robert Blau. Copyright May 11, 1986, Chicago Tribune Company, all rights reserved. Used with permission.

Excerpt on page 248 from "Puppet Theater Can Make All Our Dreams Come True" by Robert Wolf. Reprinted by permission of Chicago Tribune Company.

Excerpt on page 285 from *The Woman Warrior* by Maxine Hong Kingston. Copyright 1975, 1976 by Maxine Hong Kingston. Reprinted by permission of Alfred A. Knopf, Inc.

Excerpt on page 286 from *Rivethead*, © 1991 by Ben Hamper. Reprinted by permission of Warner Books/New York.

Folktale on page 287, "One Never Knows," from *African Folk Tales* © 1965 Peter Pauper Press. Reprinted with permission.

Excerpt on page 288 from *Their Eyes Were Watching God* by Zora Neale Hurston. Copyright 1937 by Harper & Row, Inc. Copyright renewed 1965 by John C. Hurston and Joel Hurston. Reprinted by permission of HarperCollins Publishers, Inc.

Excerpt on page 289 from "A Perfect Hotspot" by Virgil Suárez in *Welcome to the Oasis*. Reprinted with permission of the publisher, Arte Publico Press/University of Houston.

Poem on page 290, "Lament" by Edna St. Vincent Millay, in *Collected Poems*, HarperCollins. Copyright 1921, 1948 by Edna St. Vincent Millay. Reprinted by permission of Elizabeth Barnett, literary executor.

Excerpt on page 291 from *New Ice Age* by Gus Edwards. Copyright 1985 by Gus Edwards. All rights reserved. Selection used by special permission from Susan Schulman, A Literary Agency, granted on behalf of the author.

Review on page 292 reprinted with permission from *TV Guide*® magazine. Copyright 1993 by News America Publications Inc.

Excerpt on page 293 from "*Marvin's Room* Still a Winner." Copyright 1993 Chicago Tribune Company. All rights reserved. Used with permission.

The editor has made every effort to trace ownership of all copyrighted material and to secure the necessary permissions. Should there be a question regarding the use of any material, regret is hereby expressed for such error. Upon notification of any such oversight, proper acknowledgment will be made in future editions.

Photo Credits

Photo on page 12 © Michael Melford/ The Image Bank.

Photo on page 36 © Fernando Bergamaschi/The Image Bank.

Photos on pages 60, 92, 116, 162 reprinted by permission of The Bettmann Archive, UPI/Bettmann.

Photo on page 173: AP/World Wide Photo.

Photo on page 250: National Museum of American Art, Smithsonian Institution.

To the Student

If you're studying to pass the GED Tests, you're in good company. In 1992, the most recent year for which figures are available, over 790,000 people took the tests. Of this number, nearly 480,000 actually received their certificates. Why do so many people choose to take the GED Tests? Some do so to get a job or to get a better one than they already have. Others take the tests so that they can go on to college or vocational school. Still others pursue their GED diplomas to feel better about themselves or to set good examples for their children.

Americans and Canadians alike, from all walks of life, have passed their GED Tests and obtained diplomas. Some well-known graduates include country music singers Waylon Jennings and John Michael Montgomery, comedian Bill Cosby, Olympic gold medalist Mary Lou Retton, former New Jersey Governor James J. Florio, Wendy's Old-Fashioned Hamburgers founder Dave Thomas, Delaware State Senator Ruth Ann Minner, U.S. Senator Ben Nighthorse Campbell of Colorado, motion picture actor Kelly McGillis, Famous Amos Chocolate Chip Cookies creator Wally Amos, *Parade* magazine editor Walter Anderson, NBA referee Tommy Nuñez, and Triple Crown winner jockey Ron Turcotte.

This book has been designed to help you, too, succeed on the test. It will provide you with instruction in the skills you need to pass, background information on key concepts, and plenty of practice with the kinds of test items you will find on the real test.

WHAT DOES GED STAND FOR?

GED stands for the Tests of General Educational Development. The GED Test is a national examination developed by the GED Testing Service of the American Council on Education. The credential received for passing the test is widely recognized by colleges, training schools, and employers as equivalent to a high school diploma.

While the GED Test measures skills and knowledge normally acquired in four years of high school, much that you have learned informally or through other types of training can help you pass the test.

The GED Test is available in English, French, and Spanish and on audiocassette, in Braille, and in large print.

WHAT SHOULD I KNOW TO PASS THE TEST?

The test consists of five examinations in the areas of writing skills, social studies, science, literature and the arts, and mathematics. The chart on the next page outlines the main content areas, the breakdown of questions, and the time allowed per test.

THE GED TESTS			
Test	*Minutes*	*Questions*	*Percentage*
1: Writing Skills Part 1: Conventions of English	75	55	Sentence Structure 35% Usage 35% Mechanics 30%
Part 2: The Essay	45	1 topic	
2: Social Studies	85	64	History 25% Economics 20% Political Science 20% Geography 15%* Behavioral Sciences 20%*
3: Science	95	66	Life Sciences 50% Physical Sciences 50%
4: Literature and the Arts	65	45	Popular Literature 50% Classical Literature 25% Commentary 25%
5: Mathematics	90	56	Arithmetic 50% Algebra 30% Geometry 20%

*In Canada, 20% of the test is based on Geography and 15% on Behavioral Sciences.

On all five tests, you are expected to demonstrate the ability to think about many issues. You also are tested on knowledge and skills you have acquired from life experiences, television, radio, books and newspapers, consumer products, and advertising. In addition to the above information, keep these facts in mind:

1. Three of the five tests—Literature and the Arts, Science, and Social Studies— require that you answer questions based on reading passages or interpreting cartoons, diagrams, maps, charts, and graphs in these content areas. Developing strong reading and thinking skills is the key to succeeding on these tests.

2. The Writing Skills Test requires you to be able to detect and correct errors in sentence structure, grammar, punctuation, and spelling. You also will have to write a composition of approximately 200 words on a topic familiar to most adults.

3. The Mathematics Test consists mainly of word problems to be solved. Therefore, you must be able to combine your ability to perform computations with problem-solving skills.

WHO MAY TAKE THE TESTS?

In the United States, Canada, and many territories, people who have not graduated from high school and who meet specific eligibility requirements (age, residency, etc.) may take the tests. Since eligibility requirements vary, it would be useful to contact your local GED testing center or the director of adult education in your state, province, or territory for specific information.

WHAT IS A PASSING SCORE ON THE GED TEST?

Again, this varies from area to area. To find out what you need to pass the test, contact your local GED testing center. However, you must keep two scores in mind. One score represents the minimum score you must get on each test. For example, if your state requires minimum scores of 40, you must get at least 40 points on every test. Additionally, you must meet the requirements of a minimum average score on all five tests. For example, if your state requires a minimum average score of 45, you must get a total of 225 points to pass. The two scores together, the minimum score and the minimum average score, determine whether you pass or fail the GED Test.

To understand this better, look at the scores of three people who took the test in a state that requires a minimum score of 40 and a minimum average score of 45 (225 total). Ann and Willie did not pass, but Ramon did. See if you can tell why.

	Ann	Willie	Ramon
Test 1	44	42	43
Test 2	43	43	48
Test 3	38	42	47
Test 4	50	40	52
Test 5	50	40	49
	225	207	239

Ann made the total of 225 points but fell below the minimum score on Test 3. Willie passed each test but failed to get the 225 points needed; just passing the individual tests was not enough. Ramon passed all the tests and exceeded the minimum score. Generally, to receive a GED credential, you must correctly answer half or a little more than half of the questions on each test.

MAY I RETAKE THE TEST?

You are allowed to retake some or all of the tests. Again, the regulations governing the number of times that you may retake the tests and the time you must wait before retaking them are set by your state, province, or territory. Some states require you to take a review class or to study on your own for a certain amount of time before taking the test again.

HOW CAN I BEST PREPARE FOR THE TEST?

Many libraries, community colleges, adult education centers, churches, and other institutions offer GED preparation classes. Some television stations broadcast classes to prepare people for the test. If you cannot find a GED preparation class locally, contact the director of adult education in your state, province, or territory or call the GED Hotline (800-62-MY-GED). This hotline will give you telephone numbers and addresses of adult education and testing centers in your area. The hotline is staffed 24 hours a day, seven days a week.

WHAT'S ON THE LITERATURE AND THE ARTS TEST?

For the GED Literature and the Arts Test, you will read passages of literature, both fiction and nonfiction, and answer questions about them. Each passage is introduced by a *purpose question*, a question designed to help you focus your reading of a passage. Passages are about 200 to 400 words long. The questions following each passage are multiple choice.

The questions on the GED Literature and the Arts Test do *not* require you to memorize facts. To answer questions successfully, you will need to:

- understand what you read

- apply information to a new situation

- analyze elements of style and structure in passages

As an adult, you have a wealth of life experience. It's likely that your experience has helped you develop many of the reading and thinking skills you need to pass the test. By working through this book, you will further develop those skills, build new ones, and get plenty of practice applying the skills to passages of literature.

The GED Literature and the Arts Test can be broken down into the content it covers and the skills it tests. These subjects make up the content:

Popular Literature	50%
Classical Literature	25%
Commentary About Literature and the Arts	25%

Popular literature consists of outstanding contemporary fiction, nonfiction, drama, and poetry. For example, you might encounter an excerpt from a recent, well-written magazine article or a brief scene from a current, well-constructed play. *Classical literature* consists of outstanding fiction, nonfiction, drama, and poetry that has earned a place in literary history. A passage from Edith Wharton's novel *Ethan Frome* or Langston Hughes's poem

"Dream Deferred" would qualify as classical literature. **Commentary** consists of writings *about* literature and the arts. Commentary might include an excerpt from a well-written newspaper review of a movie, play, or a concert. In chapters 4–8 of this book, you will learn techniques for reading short stories, novels, plays, and poems as well as commentary and other kinds of nonfiction.

Remember that you will be asked to do more than just find an answer given in a passage. You will be tested on your ability to think about certain ideas and concepts. The thinking skills you will encounter are as follows:

Comprehending Ideas	60%
Analyzing Ideas	25%
Applying Ideas	15%

Comprehending ideas refers to the ability to understand and draw inferences, or conclusions, about a passage. *Analyzing ideas* consists of breaking a passage into logical parts and thinking about how the parts fit together. *Applying ideas* refers to the ability to take information or knowledge gained from one situation and use it to answer questions about another, similar situation. Chapters 1–3 of this book focus on these three major thinking skills. In addition, every exercise in this book is designed to help develop one or more of these skills.

When you take the test, do *not* worry about whether a passage is from popular or classical literature or about what type of thinking skill is being tested. The charts above are intended only to show you how the Literature and the Arts Test may differ from other tests you have taken.

TEST-TAKING TIPS FOR SUCCESS

1. **Prepare physically.** Get plenty of rest and eat a well-balanced meal before the test so that you will have energy and will be able to think clearly. Last-minute cramming will probably not help as much as a relaxed and rested mind.

2. **Arrive early.** Be at the testing center at least 15 to 20 minutes before the starting time. Make sure you have time to find the room and to get situated. Keep in mind that many testing centers refuse to admit latecomers.

3. **Think positively.** Tell yourself you will do well. If you have studied and prepared for the test, you should succeed.

4. **Relax during the test.** Take half a minute several times during the test to stretch and breathe deeply, especially if you are feeling anxious or confused.

5. **Read the test directions carefully.** Be sure you understand how to answer the questions. If you have any questions about the test or about filling in the answer form, ask before the test begins.

6. **Know the time limit for each test.** The Literature and the Arts Test has a time limit of 65 minutes.

   Some testing centers allow extra time, while others do not. You may be able to find out the policy of your testing center before you take the test, but always work according to the official time limit. If you have extra time, go back and check your answers.

7. **Have a strategy for answering questions.** You should read through the reading passages, or look over the pictorial materials, once and then answer the questions that follow. Read each question two or three times to make sure you understand it. It is best to refer back to the passage or illustration in order to confirm your answer choice. Don't try to depend on your memory of what you have just read or seen. Some people like to guide their reading by skimming the questions before reading a passage. Use the method that works best for you.

8. **Don't spend a lot of time on difficult questions.** If you're not sure of an answer, go on to the next question. Answer easier questions first and then go back to the harder questions. However, when you skip a question, be sure that you have skipped the same number on your answer sheet. Although skipping difficult questions is a good strategy for making the most of your time, it is very easy to get confused and throw off your whole answer key.

   Lightly mark the margin of your answer sheet next to the numbers of the questions you did not answer so that you know what to go back to. To prevent confusion when your test is graded, be sure to erase these marks completely after you answer the questions.

9. **Answer every question on the test.** If you're not sure of an answer, take an educated guess. When you leave a question unanswered, you will always lose points, but you can possibly gain points if you make a correct guess.

   If you must guess, try to eliminate one or more answers that you are sure are not correct. Then choose from the remaining answers. Remember, you greatly increase your chances if you can eliminate one or two answers before guessing. Of course, guessing should be used only when all else has failed.

10. **Clearly fill in the circle for each answer choice.** If you erase something, erase it completely. Be sure that you give only one answer per question; otherwise, no answer will count.

11. **Practice test taking.** Use the exercises, reviews, and especially the Post-Test and Practice Test in this book to better understand your test-taking habits and weaknesses. Use them to practice different strategies such as skimming questions first or skipping hard questions until the end. Knowing your own personal test-taking style is important to your success on the GED Test.

HOW TO USE THIS BOOK

If you are a student about to prepare for the GED Tests, you are to be admired. You have decided to resume an education that had been cut short. It is never easy to get back on track after you have been derailed, but, while it may not be easy, it will not be impossible. It will require determination and a lot of hard work.

This book will guide you through the types of questions you can expect to find on the Literature and the Arts Test. To answer some questions successfully, you will need to recall facts that you may have heard or read about previously. You may be surprised at what you already know about issues and events. If you read newspapers, magazines, historical novels, or travel guides, you are already on the road to success. If you do not read very much, now is the time to start. Not only will you improve your reading skills but you will also set a pattern for lifelong learning.

Before beginning this book, you should take the Pre-Test. This will give you a preview of what the Literature and the Arts Test includes, but, more important, it will help you identify which areas you need to concentrate on most. Use the chart at the end of the Pre-Test to pinpoint the types of questions you answered incorrectly and to determine what skills you need special work in. You may decide to concentrate on specific areas or to work through the entire book. We strongly suggest that you *do* work through the whole book to best prepare yourself for the actual test.

This book has a number of features designed to help make the task of test preparation easier as well as effective and enjoyable:

- A preliminary "warm-up" section of three chapters isolates the three thinking skills—*comprehension, analysis,* and *application*—and provides you with plenty of practice in applying these skills. This section includes a broad sampling of passages from all three subject areas covered on the Literature and the Arts Test. Chapters in this section are indicated by the symbol at the left.

- Content chapters cover the essential concepts that you need to know. These chapters are indicated by the symbol at the left.

- A variety of high-interest passages by popular and classic authors of diverse ethnic and cultural backgrounds are offered.

- A variety of exercise types—matching, fill-in-the-blank, true/false, multiple-choice, and short essay questions—maintain interest.

- Writing activities provide an opportunity to practice critical thinking about literature; these exercises also provide practice for the essay portion of the GED Writing Skills Test; these are indicated by the symbol at the left.

- Over 300 GED practice questions strengthen reading and thinking skills.

- An answer key (coded by skill) explains the correct answers for the exercises. If you make a mistake, you can learn from it by reading the explanation that follows the answer and then reviewing the question to analyze the error.

After you have worked through the eight chapters in this book, you should take the Post-Test. The Post-Test is a simulated GED Test that presents questions in the format, at the level of difficulty, and in the percentages found on the actual test. The Post-Test will help you determine whether you are ready for the GED Literature and the Arts Test and, if not, what areas of the book you need to review. The Post-Test evaluation chart at the end will be especially helpful for making this decision.

We realize that practice makes perfect. Therefore, we've added a Practice Test as a final indicator of your readiness for the real GED Test. This test is just like the Post-Test in terms of its format, level of difficulty, and percentages found on the real test. After you have completed the Practice Test, you will be able to finally determine whether you are ready to take the GED Test and, if not, what areas you need to review. As with the Post-Test, an evaluation chart is included to help you judge your performance.

Contemporary Books publishes a wide range of materials to help you prepare for the tests. These books are designed for home study or classroom use. Our GED preparation books are available through schools and bookstores and directly from the publisher. Our toll-free number is (800) 621-1918. For the visually impaired, a large-print version is available. For further information, call Library Reproduction Service (LRS) at (800) 255-5002.

Finally, we'd like to hear from you. If our materials have helped you to pass the test or if you feel that we can do a better job preparing you, write to us at the address on the back of the book to let us know. We hope you enjoy studying for the GED Test with our materials and wish you the greatest success.

The Editors

Literature and the Arts Pre-Test

Directions: Before you begin to work with this book, take this pre-test. The purpose of the pre-test is to help you determine which skills you need to develop to pass the GED Literature and the Arts Test.

The Literature and the Arts Pre-Test consists of twenty multiple-choice questions. These questions are based on passages of fiction and nonfiction prose, poetry, drama, and commentary on literature and the arts.

Answer each question as carefully as possible, choosing the best of five answer choices and blackening in the grid. If you find a question too difficult, do not waste time on it. Work ahead and come back to it later, when you can think it through carefully.

When you have completed the test, check your work with the answers and explanations at the end of the section.

Use the evaluation chart on page 9 to determine which areas you need to review most. For the best possible preparation for the GED Literature and the Arts Test, however, we advise you to work through this entire book.

PRE-TEST ANSWER GRID

1 ① ② ③ ④ ⑤		**8** ① ② ③ ④ ⑤		**15** ① ② ③ ④ ⑤
2 ① ② ③ ④ ⑤		**9** ① ② ③ ④ ⑤		**16** ① ② ③ ④ ⑤
3 ① ② ③ ④ ⑤		**10** ① ② ③ ④ ⑤		**17** ① ② ③ ④ ⑤
4 ① ② ③ ④ ⑤		**11** ① ② ③ ④ ⑤		**18** ① ② ③ ④ ⑤
5 ① ② ③ ④ ⑤		**12** ① ② ③ ④ ⑤		**19** ① ② ③ ④ ⑤
6 ① ② ③ ④ ⑤		**13** ① ② ③ ④ ⑤		**20** ① ② ③ ④ ⑤
7 ① ② ③ ④ ⑤		**14** ① ② ③ ④ ⑤		

Directions: Read each passage and choose the best answer to each question that follows.

Questions 1–4 refer to the following excerpt from an article.

HOW DOES IT FEEL TO BE SICK IN A FOREIGN COUNTRY?

Shotsy Faust walks into the examining room wearing casual clothes and her best bedside manner, and introduces herself to a Russian patient recently arrived in San
5 Francisco. She smiles. "Hi, nice to meet you. I'm a nurse practitioner. How are you today?" The man looks uncomfortable. He scowls and mutters to the interpreter in Russian, "Who is this fool?" Later, the
10 interpreter explains: "He thought you were a ninny because you were so friendly. Next time you have a Russian patient, try wearing a white coat and acting more formal."

It is one of the twists and turns Faust
15 has become accustomed to as director of San Francisco General Hospital's bustling refugee clinic; one of the hazards of stepping into a different world each time she greets a new patient, moving seamlessly
20 from Saigon to Ethiopia to Baghdad to Cuba to a small village in the hills of Laos. A Haitian man refuses a blood test, fearing that the blood, which holds part of the soul, might be used for sorcery. A Vietnamese
25 patient cuts his medication in half, convinced that American drugs, meant for large people, will be too strong. A Cambodian woman's family does not want her to die at home: her spirit, they insist, will
30 linger in the apartment after her death.

In clinics and emergency rooms across the country, Western medical science is colliding headlong with the beliefs and practices of other cultures as a new wave of
35 migration turns even many a suburban hospital into a small United Nations. In 1992, more than 1 million legal immigrants and refugees entered the United States. Most of the newcomers speak little or no English.

40 Many regard doctors with exaggerated awe, distrust or a mixture of the two. And more than a few carry the scars of horrifying experiences—rape, torture, imprisonment, slaughter of family members—experiences
45 making them prime candidates for both physical and psychological illness.

This multicultural flood is changing the way health workers practice their profession, creating a surge of interest in cross-cultural
50 research and challenging American medicine's traditional ethnocentrism. In Boston and Fresno, Minneapolis and Miami, a growing number of hospitals are hiring full-time interpreters for significant patient
55 minorities, providing training for staff in cultural differences and even adding ethnic foods to their menus.

—Excerpted from "The Cultures of Illness," *U.S. News & World Report*, February 15, 1993

1. Shotsy Faust is a

   (1) representative to the United Nations
   (2) director of a hospital refugee clinic
   (3) foreign language expert specializing in Russian
   (4) Cambodian woman who is dying
   (5) Russian doctor who understands her patients

2. The excerpt is mainly about how

   (1) U.S. hospitals are trying to meet the special needs of immigrant patients
   (2) patients from other countries are traveling to the United States for health care
   (3) a U.S. doctor is struggling to get along with her immigrant patients
   (4) patients from other countries dislike and distrust U.S. doctors
   (5) immigrant patients tend to ignore U.S. doctors' orders and prescriptions

3. What does the author mean when she says in lines 34–36 that "a new wave of migration [is] turn[ing] even many a suburban hospital into a small United Nations"?

   (1) Small suburban hospitals are becoming more like big-city hospitals.
   (2) Suburban hospital workers are learning to solve problems in democratic ways.
   (3) Suburban hospitals are treating increasing numbers of newcomers to the United States.
   (4) Suburban hospitals are not equipped to treat patients who do not speak English.
   (5) Hospitalized suburbanites are forming close friendships with patients from other nations.

4. What advice might Shotsy Faust give to health care workers who treat minority patients?

   (1) Make the patients feel comfortable by acting casual and friendly.
   (2) Write instructions clearly to make them easy for patients to follow.
   (3) Speak loudly and carefully to ensure that the patients understand you.
   (4) Improve communication by showing respect for the beliefs of the patients.
   (5) Dress in white clothing to warn the patients that you are a medical doctor.

Questions 5–8 refer to the following excerpt from a novel.

WHAT DO YOU NOTICE ABOUT HUCK'S RELATIONSHIP WITH HIS FATHER?

As for his clothes—just rags, that was all. He had one ankle resting on t'other knee; the boot on that foot was busted, and two of his toes stuck through, and he
5 worked them now and then. His hat was laying on the floor—an old black slouch with the top caved in, like a lid.

I stood a-looking at him; he set there a-looking at me, with his chair tilted back a
10 little. I set the candle down. I noticed the window was up; so he had clumb in by the shed. He kept a-looking me all over. By and by he says:

"Starchy clothes—very. You think you're
15 a good deal of a big-bug, *don't* you?"

"Maybe I am, maybe I ain't," I says.

"Don't you give me none o' your lip," says he. "You've put on considerable many frills since I been away. I'll take you down a
20 peg before I get done with you. You're educated, too, they say—can read and write. You think you're better'n your father, now, don't you, because he can't? *I'll* take it out of you. Who told you you might meddle with
25 such hifalut'n foolishness, hey?—who told you you could?"

"The widow. She told me."

"The widow, hey?—and who told the widow she could put in her shovel about a
30 thing that ain't none of her business?"

"Nobody never told her."

"Well, I'll learn her how to meddle. And looky here—you drop that school, you hear? I'll learn people to bring up a boy to put on
35 airs over his own father and let on to be better'n what *he* is. You lemme catch you fooling around that school again, you hear? Your mother couldn't read, and she couldn't write, nuther, before she died. None of the
40 family couldn't before *they* died. *I* can't; and here you're a-swelling yourself up like this. I ain't the man to stand it—you hear?"

—Mark Twain, excerpted from *Adventures of Huckleberry Finn*, 1884

5. The phrases "a-looking" (lines 8 and 9) and "clumb in" (line 11) tell you that the narrator of the story

(1) doesn't get along with his father
(2) speaks a foreign language
(3) speaks standard English
(4) cannot read or write
(5) speaks in dialect

6. What is the main topic of conversation between Huck and his father?

(1) the widow's meddling
(2) Huck's education
(3) the mother's death
(4) the family's background
(5) Huck's father's behavior

7. The purpose of the dialogue is to

(1) explain why sons should obey their fathers
(2) reveal some of the problems of a single parent
(3) imply that Huck and his father should study grammar
(4) dramatize the conflict between Huck and his father
(5) make fun of Huck's and his father's upbringings

8. What social problem discussed in this excerpt is also being addressed today?

(1) illiteracy
(2) child abuse
(3) alcoholism
(4) juvenile delinquency
(5) kidnapping

Questions 9–12 refer to the following poem.

HOW DOES A LANDLORD REACT TO HIS TENANT?

Ballad of the Landlord

Landlord, landlord,
My roof has sprung a leak.
Don't you 'member I told you about it
Way last week?

5   Landlord, landlord,
These steps is broken down.
When you come up yourself
It's a wonder you don't fall down.

Ten Bucks you say I owe you?
10   Ten Bucks you say is due?
Well, that's Ten Bucks more'n I'll pay you
Till you fix this house up new.

What? You gonna get eviction orders?
You gonna cut off my heat?
15   You gonna take my furniture and
Throw it in the street?

Um-huh! You talking high and mighty.
Talk on—till you get through.
You ain't gonna be able to say a word
20   If I land my fist on you.

Police! Police!
Come and get this man!
He's trying to ruin the government
And overturn the land!

25   Copper's whistle!
Patrol bell!
Arrest.

Precinct Station.
Iron cell.
Headlines in press:

30   MAN THREATENS LANDLORD

•
• •

TENANT HELD NO BAIL

•
• •

JUDGE GIVES NEGRO 90 DAYS IN COUNTY JAIL

—Langston Hughes, 1951

9. Stanza 6 (lines 21–24) is told from whose point of view? The

(1) landlord's
(2) tenant's
(3) poet's
(4) bill collector's
(5) janitor's

10. You can conclude that the landlord is

(1) hot-tempered
(2) conscientious
(3) friendly
(4) negligent
(5) poor

11. The landlord threatens to evict the tenant because the tenant

(1) turned off the heat
(2) destroyed the stairwell
(3) threw the furniture on the street
(4) caused the roof to leak
(5) refused to pay $10

12. The tenant's language in the first four stanzas (lines 1–16) most closely resembles

(1) an apartment lease
(2) a complaint letter
(3) an eviction notice
(4) a police report
(5) a newspaper story

Questions 13–16 refer to the following excerpt from a play.

HOW DO TONY AND RIFF FEEL ABOUT A GANG CALLED THE JETS?

TONY: Now go play nice with the Jets.

RIFF: The Jets are the greatest!

TONY: Were.

RIFF: Are. You found somethin' better?

5 TONY: No. But—

RIFF: But what?

TONY: You won't dig it.

RIFF: Try me.

TONY: O.K. . . . Every single damn night for
10 the last month, I wake up—and I'm
reachin' out.

RIFF: For what?

TONY: I don't know. It's right outside
the door, around the corner. But
15 it's comin'!

RIFF: *What* is? Tell me!

TONY: I don't know! It's—like the kick I
used to get from bein' a Jet.

RIFF: . . . Or from bein' buddies.

20 TONY: We're still buddies.

RIFF: The kick comes from people,
buddy boy.

TONY: Yeah, but not from being a Jet.

RIFF: No? Without a gang you're an
25 orphan. With a gang you walk in
twos, threes, fours. And when your
gang is the best, when you're a Jet,
buddy boy, you're out in the sun and
home free home!

30 TONY: Riff, I've had it. *[Pause]*

RIFF: Tony, the trouble is large: the Sharks
bite hard! We got to stop them now,
and we need *you*! *[Pause. Quietly]* I
never asked the time of day from a
35 clock, but I'm askin' you: Come to
the dance tonight . . . *[TONY turns
away]* . . . I already told the gang
you'd be there.

TONY: *[After a moment, turns to him with a
40 grin]* What time?

RIFF: Ten?

TONY: Ten it is.

—Arthur Laurents and Leonard Bernstein,
excerpted from *West Side Story*, 1957

13. The word *kick* (lines 17 and 21) refers to a

(1) football punt
(2) drug-induced sensation
(3) thrilling experience
(4) sum of money
(5) leg movement

14. Why does Riff say, "Without a gang you're an orphan" (lines 24–25)? To

(1) suggest that Tony's parents are dead
(2) analyze why city kids feel abandoned
(3) imply that Tony's parents ignore him
(4) compare a gang to a family
(5) show that gangs recruit orphans

15. What is Riff's tone of voice when he asks Tony to go to the dance?

(1) mean
(2) pleading
(3) angry
(4) bossy
(5) sad

16. Tony decides to attend the dance because he

(1) is excited about being in a gang
(2) hasn't gone out for the last month
(3) wants to find a girlfriend
(4) doesn't have anything better to do
(5) values his friendship with Riff

Questions 17–20 refer to the following excerpt from a commentary on the arts.

WHAT IS IT LIKE TO BE NOMINATED FOR AN OSCAR?

It's a full-time job that's offered to certain qualified actors every February and hardly ever turned down: Oscar nominee. The requirements are relatively simple. You
5 spend the next two months or so grinning appreciatively; praising the other nominees; assuring interviewers that it doesn't really matter who wins, just being nominated is such an honor; deflecting credit from
10 yourself to the director, the costumer, the makeup person, your agent; and confronting daily ads in the trade journals that offer up your face for the reader's "consideration," as if someone might wish to add a mustache or
15 fix your nose.

If you're a dark horse, you bask, certain that when you begin your acceptance speech with the time-honored boilerplate— "Wow, I really wasn't expecting this"—you'll
20 be believed. If you're running in the middle of the pack, you grow unexpectedly religious; there are no atheists at the Nominees Luncheon (held at the Beverly Hilton Hotel a couple of weeks before the
25 ceremony). And if you're regarded as a shoo-in (Al Pacino, Emma Thompson) your life becomes a series of bizarre psychological rituals. You find yourself thinking that for perhaps the first time in its
30 history the Academy has chosen well: have there ever been so many fabulous performances in a single year? You pray that when your big moment comes you'll remember whom to thank, because while
35 the rest of the world is wincing at every fresh expression of gratitude all the people you've ever worked with are swearing vengeance if they don't hear their names. And you make invisible deals, vowing to give
40 up smoking, to sacrifice on-the-set trysts with co-stars, to donate your screening room to the homeless, if only, just this once, the gods will let you win.

—Stephen Schiff, excerpted from "To Be a Nominee," *The New Yorker*, March 22, 1993

17. The details in the second paragraph are organized in categories to

(1) explain the process of choosing Academy Award nominees
(2) tell about the different types of awards given each year by the academy
(3) describe how different candidates behave during the months before Oscar night
(4) contrast the reactions of nominees who win with those who lose
(5) trace the history and development of the Academy Awards ceremonies

18. According to the excerpt, a benefit of being a dark-horse nominee is that

(1) interviewers assure you that it doesn't matter if you win
(2) trade journals print flattering photographs of you
(3) your director, makeup person, and agent take credit for your success
(4) members of the academy hold a special luncheon for you
(5) people believe your surprise is genuine when you win

19. The writer regards the anxiety of the Oscar nominees as

(1) humorous and melodramatic
(2) emotional and draining
(3) immature and childlike
(4) spiritual and sobering
(5) healthful and realistic

20. Imagine that you are a photographer taking pictures of the Nominees Luncheon. Which picture would capture the main idea of the excerpt best?

(1) the actors displaying the costumes they wore in the roles they were nominated for
(2) the nominees giving phony smiles of encouragement to each other
(3) the attendees sitting down to eat a fancy meal in a richly decorated hall
(4) the winners making tearful speeches to the academy
(5) TV reporters interviewing the stars while fans line up for autographs

PRE-TEST

ANSWERS BEGIN ON PAGE 8.

Pre-Test Answer Key

1. **(2)** Lines 15–17 say that Faust is director of San Francisco General Hospital's refugee clinic.

2. **(1)** Throughout the excerpt, statements point out the main idea that "Western medical science is colliding headlong with the beliefs and practices of other cultures" (lines 32–34) and that "this multicultural flood is changing the way health workers practice their profession" (lines 47–48).

3. **(3)** The entire excerpt describes how hospitals are dealing with the increasing need to understand people of cultural backgrounds as diverse as the member countries of the United Nations.

4. **(4)** As director of a refugee clinic, Faust is sensitive to the needs of people of other cultures.

5. **(5)** Huck, the narrator, speaks a regional English dialect that differs from standard English. You know from the passage that Huck and his father do not get along, yet that is unrelated to Huck's manner of speech. Lines 20–21 clearly state that Huck knows how to read and write.

6. **(2)** The focus of their discussion is the father's reaction to Huck's education.

7. **(4)** The dialogue dramatizes the conflict between Huck and his father. Huck's father is strongly opposed to Huck's schooling.

8. **(1)** In the concluding paragraph, the father states that no one in the family could read or write. Today, many Americans are also illiterate.

9. **(1)** You can conclude that the landlord is responding to the tenant's threats. In lines 19–20, the tenant tells the landlord, "You ain't gonna be able to say a word / If I land my fist on you." As a result, the landlord calls, *"Police! Police! / Come and get this man!"*

10. **(4)** According to the tenant, the landlord hasn't repaired the leaking roof or the broken steps. Therefore, you can conclude that the landlord is negligent.

11. **(5)** In lines 9–12, the tenant states that he refuses to pay "Ten Bucks" until the landlord fixes "this house up new." The landlord apparently believes that this overdue payment is grounds for eviction.

12. **(2)** As a person would do in a complaint letter, the tenant directly states his grievances.

13. **(3)** Tony and Riff use the word *kick* figuratively, not literally. The kick from belonging to a gang or being with people refers to a thrilling experience.

14. **(4)** Riff is indirectly comparing a gang to a family. He is suggesting that the bond among gang members is similar to the bond among blood relatives. He is saying that not belonging to a gang is like being an orphan.

15. **(2)** Riff's request that Tony attend the dance is urgent.

16. **(5)** In line 20, Tony says to Riff, "We're still buddies." You can conclude that Tony's decision to attend the dance is a personal favor to Riff.

17. **(3)** In paragraph 2, the author describes how dark-horse, middle-of-the-pack, and shoo-in candidates behave as they wait for Oscar night.

18. **(5)** At the beginning of paragraph 2, the author states that "you'll be believed" if you begin your acceptance speech by saying, "Wow, I really wasn't expecting this."

19. **(1)** The author uses good-natured satire to overdramatize the nominees' worries.

20. **(2)** According to the excerpt, each nominee inwardly hopes to win while outwardly "praising the other nominees" (line 6).

Pre-Test Evaluation Chart

Use the chart below to determine the reading skills areas in which you need to do the most work. For the GED Literature and the Arts Test, you are required to answer the following types of questions: literal comprehension (global and specific), inferential comprehension (global and specific), analysis, and application. These reading skills, covered on pages 13–89 of this book, are absolutely essential for success on the test. Circle any items that you got wrong and pay particular attention to areas where you missed half or more of the questions.

Skill Area/ Content Area	Literal Comprehension	Inferential Comprehension	Analysis	Application
Nonfiction Prose (pages 93–115)	1, 2	3		4
Prose Fiction (pages 117–161)		6	5, 7	8
Poetry (pages 163–193)		10, 11	9	12
Drama (pages 195–227)	13	14, 15, 16		
Commentaries on the Arts (pages 229–265)	18	19	17	20

Questions 10–13 refer to the following excerpt from a book about workers.

WHAT DO YOU NOTICE ABOUT COAL MINERS?

When the miner comes up from the pit his face is so pale that it is noticeable even through the mask of coal dust. This is due to the foul air that he has been breathing, and
5   will wear off presently. To a Southerner, new to the mining districts, the spectacle of a shift of several hundred miners streaming out of the pit is strange and slightly sinister. Their exhausted faces, with the grime
10 clinging in all the hollows, have a fierce, wild look. At other times, when their faces are clean, there is not much to distinguish them from the rest of the population. They have a very upright square-shouldered walk, a
15 reaction from the constant bending underground, but most of them are shortish men and their thick ill-fitting clothes hide the splendor of their bodies. The most definitely distinctive thing about them is the blue scars
20 on their noses. Every miner has blue scars on his nose and forehead, and will carry them to his death. The coal dust of which the air underground is full enters every cut, and then the skin grows over it and forms a
25 blue stain like tattooing, which in fact it is. Some of the older men have their foreheads veined like Roquefort cheeses from this cause.

—George Orwell, excerpted from
The Road to Wigan Pier, 1937

10. The purpose of this passage is to

(1) explain the dangers of coal mining
(2) tell why miners are exhausted after work
(3) describe how a coal miner looks
(4) detail the way a coal miner walks
(5) warn miners to watch their health

11. According to the passage, the miners' faces are pale when they leave the coal pit because the men

(1) are tired from working hard
(2) were breathing foul air
(3) aren't exposed to enough sunlight
(4) want to look strange and sinister
(5) feel faint from the heat

12. Why do miners have permanent scars on their noses and foreheads?

(1) They always bang their heads against the low ceiling of the coal pit.
(2) They all tattoo their noses and foreheads with blue ink.
(3) Their noses and foreheads are covered with bluish-black coal dust.
(4) They bruise themselves when they are shoveling coal.
(5) Blue-stained skin forms over the coal miners' cuts.

13. Based on the passage, you can tell that the word *Roquefort* in line 27 refers to

(1) a growth on the skin
(2) the medical term for a wound
(3) the name of a coal-mining town
(4) a type of cheese
(5) a muscular pain

ANSWERS ARE ON PAGE 297.

Fictional detective Sherlock Holmes is famous for his powers of observation and ability to make inferences based on clues. Effective readers share these skills.

2 Inferential Understanding

Inferential understanding is a way of thinking—a reasoning process you use to help you interpret your experiences. When you make an *inference*, you draw upon what you observe and know. Based on your observations and knowledge, you make an educated guess about the meaning of your experience.

This chapter will help you build your reading skills in inferential understanding. You will learn how to:

- use supporting details to make an inference
- make sure your inferences are valid
- interpret figurative language

MAKING INFERENCES

You are driving along a main street. As you near the railroad tracks, you notice two flashing red lights. Bells clang as you watch the crossing gates fall, stopping traffic. You hear a distant whistle.

What would you infer about this situation? You would probably conclude that a train is approaching. Why? Certain clues guided your thinking. Flashing red lights, clanging bells, falling crossing gates, a distant whistle—all these clues hinted that a train was approaching.

Based upon your observations and knowledge, you made an educated guess. You assumed your inference was correct, although nobody told you directly. Actually seeing the train speeding by would prove that you were right.

The inferences that you make depend largely upon your powers of observation—your ability to spot important details or clues. The next example illustrates how specific clues support an inference:

Observation: A man wearing dark glasses taps his cane against the pavement. His German shepherd leads him across an alley.

Inference: The man is blind.

Clues: 1. Wears dark glasses
2. Walks with a cane
3. Is directed by a German shepherd, probably trained as a Seeing Eye dog

EXERCISE 1

Directions: Apply your skills in detecting clues that support inferences. Carefully study the observations. Then list the clues that show why the inference for each observation is valid.

1. Observation: During the second quarter of a football game, the referee blows his whistle. The tackled quarterback lies motionless on the field. Two men with a stretcher rush from the sidelines and carry him away.

Inference: The quarterback is injured.

Clues: _____

2. Observation: A job seeker receives a message asking that she call the Human Resources Department of a company where she interviewed for a job. When she calls, the director says, "Congratulations!"

Inference: The director is extending a job offer.

Clues: _____

3. Observation: As a woman walks toward the door of a small clothing store, a high-pitched alarm goes off. The store manager races after the woman and grabs her arm. A sweater, stuffed inside the woman's coat, drops to the floor.

Inference: The manager caught the woman shoplifting.

Clues: _____

4. Observation: After a concert, people in the audience loudly clap their hands and cheer. Some stand and yell, "Bravo! Bravo!"

Inference: The audience enjoyed the performance.

Clues: _____

5. Observation: A black limousine heads a long line of cars moving steadily through traffic. Although it is early afternoon, all the car headlights are on.

Inference: These cars are part of a funeral procession.

Clues: _____

ANSWERS ARE ON PAGE 298.

DRAWING VALID INFERENCES

In your own experiences, you probably make inferences automatically. You form first impressions about the people you meet. You might make assumptions about what life is like in a city, a suburb, or a small town. However, once you have made an inference, do you check its accuracy? Do you ask yourself, "Is there enough evidence to support the conclusion I have drawn? Have I overlooked any facts?" It is all too easy to draw faulty inferences.

For example, on Halloween Eve, 1938, hundreds of Americans made the same faulty inference. On that evening, the CBS Mercury Theater on Air presented a radio broadcast entitled "War of the Worlds." The script was adapted from an H. G. Wells science fiction novel. The famous actor Orson Welles told the story of an invasion from the planet Mars. Posing as an announcer, he told listeners that he had a "grave announcement." Then he proceeded to say, "Both the observations of science and the evidence of our eyes lead to the inescapable assumption that those strange beings who landed in the Jersey farmlands tonight are the vanguard of an invading army from the planet Mars."

Because the dramatic interpretation sounded real, hundreds of Americans panicked, convinced that Martians were actually destroying the country.

These people mistakenly assumed the truth of the broadcast. They feared that their lives were in danger. Yet they didn't check to find out whether their assumptions were based on fact.

How could they have avoided jumping to a hasty conclusion?

- Listeners heard Orson Welles say, "Within two hours three million people moved out of New York." This statement was an important clue. It is impossible for a city to be cleared out so quickly.

- Reading the newspaper listing of radio programs would have proved that CBS *scheduled* "War of the Worlds" to be broadcast on October 30.

- By turning the radio dial, the listeners would have discovered that the show was not an authentic broadcast. Had it been authentic, they would have heard this "national crisis" reported on other stations.

- During intermissions, the CBS radio announcer reminded the audience that they were listening to a drama.

What can you learn from this example? One important lesson is that you should understand all the facts before you make an inference.

The same word of advice applies to your reading skills. You need to build *both* literal and inferential understanding. These two skills are closely connected. Discovering the literal meaning of a passage requires you to identify what the author says directly—ideas, factual content, and supporting details. Once you have grasped the stated ideas and facts, you will want to explore what the author says indirectly—the implied or unstated meaning.

INFERRING THE UNSTATED MAIN IDEA

In the last chapter, you learned that the main idea expresses the central message of a passage. Sometimes, authors will suggest the main idea rather than state it directly. In other words, the main idea is implied, and you must infer the major point based on the information given.

The following suggestions will help you infer the unstated main idea:

1. Read the passage for its literal meaning. What ideas are stated directly?

2. Read between the lines. What do the stated facts and details seem to show? How are they related? Why did the author include these facts and details?

3. Ask yourself, "What is the author suggesting about a person, a place, an event, or a belief?"

Use these guidelines as you read the following passage:

> After the game, the Crushers, a football team, slowly return to the locker room. There are no television camera operators shooting postgame highlights, no photographers popping flash bulbs, no sportscasters conducting exclusive interviews.
>
> The media are all in the opposing team's locker room. The Crushers, too exhausted to shower, sit on wooden benches. They hold their heads down and stare blankly at the floor. No one speaks. The coach bangs his fist against a locker and storms into his office, slamming the door.

Can you infer the main idea of this passage? Though the author does not state it directly, a main idea is clearly implied. To infer the point of the passage, answer the questions below.

1. Why are the camera operators, the photographers, and the sportscasters in the opposing team's locker room?

_____

_____

2. Why are the Crushers silent? How do team members' gestures and reactions reveal their emotions?

_____

_____

3. Based on the coach's behavior, what can you infer about his feelings?

_____

_____

1. The camera operators, photographers, and sportscasters are in the winning team's locker room. 2. The description of the losing players' silence and gestures suggests that they are depressed. 3. The description of the coach's behavior suggests that he is upset. By adding these clues together, you should be able to make an inference about the main idea. The author is showing you the team's reaction after losing a game. All the details contribute to the main idea. The author does not directly state, "The team is unhappy about the defeat." Yet you can infer this meaning from your answers to the preceding questions.

WRITING ACTIVITY 1

Choose one of the emotions from the list below. Then, on another piece of paper, write a description of a person displaying the emotion you chose. Do _not_ directly state what the emotion is. Instead, imply the emotion by using plenty of descriptive details. When you are finished, give your description to someone else and ask the person to guess what emotion is being described.

- terror

- joy

- grief

- excitement

ANSWERS WILL VARY.

Inferring a main idea is similar to solving a riddle. You discover the major point of a reading selection by adding up certain clues and piecing together bits of information. Your inference is a generalization that expresses the underlying meaning of these details—what all of them have in common.

Infer the main idea as you read the following excerpt, a conversation between two fictional characters. What point is General Zaroff, an expert hunter, trying to get across to Rainsford?

The general smiled the quiet smile of one who has faced an obstacle and surmounted it with success. "I had to invent a new animal to hunt," he said.

"A new animal? You're joking."

"Not at all," said the general. "I never joke about hunting. I needed a new animal. I found one. So I bought this island, built this house, and here I do my hunting. The island is perfect for my purposes—there are jungles with a maze of trails in them, hills, swamps—"

"But the animal, General Zaroff?"

"Oh," said the general, "it supplies me with the most exciting hunting in the world. No other hunting compares with it for an instant. Every day I hunt, and I never grow bored now, for I have a quarry with which I can match my wits."

Rainsford's bewilderment showed in his face.

"I wanted the ideal animal to hunt," explained the general.

"So I said: 'What are the attributes of an ideal quarry?' And the answer was, of course: 'It must have courage, cunning, and above all, it must be able to reason.' "

"But no animal can reason," objected Rainsford.

"My dear fellow," said the general, "there is one that can."

"But you can't mean—" gasped Rainsford.

"And why not?"

"I can't believe you are serious, General Zaroff. This is a grisly joke."

"Why should I not be serious? I am speaking of hunting."

"Hunting? Good God, General Zaroff, what you speak of is murder."

—Excerpted from "The Most Dangerous Game"
by Richard Connell

Here is the subject of this dialogue restated as a riddle: What animal is never boring and most exciting to hunt?

You are correct if you said, "a human being." Now expand this answer into the main idea of the passage: "General Zaroff explains to Rainsford that he has found the ideal animal to hunt—a human being." Did you notice that General Zaroff's spoken words create suspense? Rather than making straightforward remarks, he drops hints. Both Rainsford and you, the reader, have to infer his intended meaning.

WRITING ACTIVITY 2

You often form impressions about people from what they say aloud. On a separate sheet of paper, write a short paragraph describing either Zaroff or Rainsford. Quote some of the phrases and sentences that the character uses, and describe what his spoken words suggest about his outlook on life.

ANSWERS WILL VARY.

EXERCISE 2

Directions: Read each passage below and answer the questions that follow.

PASSAGE 1

Now there were no fish in the river. There were no deep potholes where fish could live. I had not been mistaken as I rode the bus, thinking that the rivers were shallower than I remembered them. The Poor Fork now was not only low; it was apparently the local refuse dump. Tin cans, pop bottles, and discarded automobile tires lined the banks, while the river itself was full of debris which it apparently was too sluggish to move along.

—Excerpted from *My Appalachia: A Reminiscence*
by Rebecca Caudill

1. Which of the following statements best summarizes the main idea?

   (1) The river moves slowly.
   (2) The trash in the river is an eyesore.
   (3) People no longer go fishing.
   (4) The river is being destroyed by pollution.
   (5) People should dump their trash in garbage cans.

2. What clues in the paragraph support your answer? On the lines, list the descriptive details that you used as evidence.

   _____

   _____

PASSAGE 2

A man stood upon a railroad bridge in northern Alabama, looking down into the swift water twenty feet below. The man's hands were tied behind his back, the wrists bound with a cord. A rope closely encircled his neck. It was attached to a stout cross-timber above his head and the slack fell to the level of his knees.

—Excerpted from "An Occurrence at Owl Creek Bridge"
by Ambrose Bierce

3. The purpose of this paragraph is to

(1) show a man about to be hanged
(2) describe the scenery of northern Alabama
(3) explain the size of a railroad bridge
(4) illustrate the uses of a rope
(5) tell about a man held hostage

4. What clues in the paragraph support your answer?

_____

_____

_____

ANSWERS ARE ON PAGE 298.

DRAWING CONCLUSIONS FROM DETAILS

You have already observed how supporting details are clues to discovering the main idea. These details also serve another purpose. Drawing conclusions from supporting details enables you to interpret the passage. Certain phrases and sentences hint at information that is not directly stated. From these specific details, you can draw conclusions about a person, a place, or a situation.

What inferences can you make about the next paragraph?

In walks these three girls in nothing but bathing suits. I'm in the third checkout slot, with my back to the door, so I don't see them until they're over by the bread. The one that caught my eye first was the one in the plaid green two-piece. She was a chunky kid, with a good tan and a sweet broad soft-looking can with those two crescents of white just under it, where the sun never seems to hit, at the top of the backs of her legs. I stood there with my hand on a box of HiHo crackers trying to remember if I rang it up or not. I ring it up again and the customer starts giving me hell. She's one of those cash-register-watchers, a witch about fifty with rouge on her cheekbones and no eyebrows, and I know it made her day to trip me up.

—Excerpted from "A & P" by John Updike

Identify the clues that support each of the following inferences:

1. The story takes place in a supermarket.

Clues: _____

2. The weather outside is hot.

Clues: _____

3. The person telling the story is a teenage boy.

Clues: _____

4. The boy is distracted by one of the girls.

Clues: _____

5. The checkout boy views the customer as an ugly, nasty-looking woman who enjoys complaining.

Clues: _____

Here are supporting details that provide clues for the inferences above:

1. References to "checkout slot," "cash register," "HiHo crackers," and "bread" suggest that the story takes place in a supermarket.

2. The girls are wearing bathing suits.

3. His speech and his interest in the girls suggest that he is a teenage boy.

4. He has observed every detail about the girl's physical appearance. He was so distracted by her that he made a mistake ringing up groceries.

5. By saying the woman is a "witch" and describing her face, the boy implies that she is ugly and nasty. His statement "I know it made her day to trip me up" suggests that the customer enjoys complaining.

Notice how much information you were able to infer from the supporting details. What if the author had decided to report all this information directly? Read the following version:

> I am a teenage boy who works as a cashier in a supermarket. One hot day three girls wearing bathing suits walked into the store. I was so distracted by the girl wearing the two-piece that I made a mistake ringing up a customer's groceries. Although the customer started complaining, I didn't really care. She looked and acted like a mean old witch.

This paragraph is obviously less interesting to read. One reason authors suggest rather than state ideas is to get the reader more interested.

GED Practice
EXERCISE 3

Read the passage below and choose the best answer to each question that follows.

WHAT DOES BLAKE FEEL?

When Blake stepped out of the elevator,
he saw her. A few people, mostly men
waiting for girls, stood in the lobby watching
the elevator doors. She was among them. As
5 he saw her, her face took on a look of such
loathing and purpose that he realized she
had been waiting for him. He did not
approach her. She had no legitimate
business with him. They had nothing to say.
10 He turned and walked toward the glass
doors at the end of the lobby, feeling that
faint guilt and bewilderment we experience
when we by-pass some old friend or
classmate who seems threadbare, or sick, or
15 miserable in some other way. It was five-
eighteen by the clock in the Western Union
office. He could catch the express. As he
waited his turn at the revolving doors, he
saw that it was still raining. It had been
20 raining all day, and he noticed now how
much louder the rain made the noises of the
street. Outside, he started walking briskly
east toward Madison Avenue. Traffic was
tied up, and horns were blowing urgently on
25 a crosstown street in the distance. The
sidewalk was crowded.

—John Cheever, excerpted from
"The Five-Forty-Eight," 1958

1. What place is Blake leaving?

   (1) a department store
   (2) an office building
   (3) a train station
   (4) a high-rise apartment
   (5) a movie theater

2. Who could the woman in the lobby be?

   (1) a stranger
   (2) an old classmate
   (3) a casual acquaintance
   (4) Blake's ex-wife
   (5) an elevator operator

3. How does Blake feel about the woman?

   (1) sick
   (2) uneasy
   (3) comfortable
   (4) impatient
   (5) happy

4. The story takes place in a

   (1) city
   (2) small town
   (3) suburb
   (4) foreign country
   (5) dangerous neighborhood

ANSWERS ARE ON PAGE 298.

DRAWING CONCLUSIONS ABOUT PEOPLE

Authors often write about people and their relationships—either real or imagined. Through descriptive details, authors suggest what a person is like. One way of revealing a person's character is to show how someone else feels about that person's behavior. As you read the next passage, what can you conclude about the girl and her mother's feelings about her?

EXERCISE 4

Directions: Read the passage below. Then complete the exercise by putting a check mark (✓) next to each statement that is a valid conclusion (one that can be supported by details in the passage).

One night I had to look at a page from the Bible for three minutes and then report everything I could remember. "Now Jehoshaphat had riches and honor in abundance and . . . that's all I remember, Ma," I said.

And after seeing my mother's disappointed face once again, something inside of me began to die. I hated the tests, the raised hopes and failed expectations. Before going to bed that night, I looked in the mirror above the bathroom sink and when I saw only my face staring back—and that it would always be this ordinary face—I began to cry. Such a sad, ugly girl! I made high-pitched noises like a crazed animal, trying to scratch out the face in the mirror.

And then I saw what seemed to be the prodigy side of me—because I had never seen that face before. I looked at my reflection, blinking so I could see more clearly. The girl staring back at me was angry, powerful. This girl and I were the same. I had new thoughts, willful thoughts, or rather thoughts filled with lots of won'ts. I won't let her change me, I promised myself. I won't be what I'm not.

—Excerpted from "Two Kinds" in *The Joy Luck Club* by Amy Tan

_____ **1.** The girl knows that her mother accepts her the way she is.

_____ **2.** The girl promises herself that she will make every effort to please her mother.

_____ **3.** The girl enjoys memorizing passages from the Bible.

_____ **4.** The girl changes from feeling sad to feeling powerful.

_____ **5.** The girl decides to be true to herself.

ANSWERS ARE ON PAGE 298.

INTERPRETING FIGURATIVE LANGUAGE

Words can be defined literally: A *graveyard* is a cemetery, a place where dead people are buried. A *bomb* is an exploding weapon that causes destruction. Words can also have figurative meanings: A mail sorter works the *graveyard* shift at the post office. Theater critics say that a certain Broadway musical is a *bomb*.

According to the literal definitions of *graveyard* and *bomb*, the preceding two sentences do not make sense. A mail sorter's job is unrelated to cemetery work. A musical is not a destructive weapon. *Graveyard* and *bomb* are used as figurative language—words that mean something other than their literal definitions. Here's a translation of both sentences into literal language—words that directly express a factual meaning:

1. A mail sorter assigned to the graveyard shift works from midnight to 8:00 A.M. at the post office.

2. Theater critics who say that a certain Broadway musical is a bomb mean that it is a complete failure.

Did you notice that the figurative language is more colorful and vivid than the literal language? Figurative language appeals to your imagination—your ability to understand the creative power of words. When you search for the figurative meaning of an expression, be aware of what the words suggest. What imaginative associations can you infer from the figurative meaning?

You use figurative language in your everyday speech. Here is an example:

Statement: "My new car is a lemon."

Literal Meaning: "My new car is a yellow, sour-tasting piece of fruit."

Figurative Meaning: "My new car is constantly breaking down."

Figures of speech often make comparisons—direct or implied—between two different things. Sometimes figurative language intentionally exaggerates or distorts the truth to emphasize a feeling or an idea.

The next two exercises will help you build your skills in understanding the differences between literal and figurative language.

EXERCISE 5

Directions: Match the figurative expression shown on the left with the correct meaning shown on the right by writing the correct letter in the space provided.

Figurative Expressions

_____ **1.** puppy love

_____ **2.** penny-pincher

_____ **3.** monkey business

_____ **4.** paint the town red

_____ **5.** tearjerker

_____ **6.** hothead

_____ **7.** sitting duck

_____ **8.** ghost ballots

_____ **9.** smash hit

_____ **10.** star

Meanings

(a) an outstanding athlete or performer

(b) celebrate wildly

(c) an easy target

(d) a teenage romance

(e) votes cast using dead people's names

(f) a sad story or performance that makes you cry

(g) a person with a bad temper

(h) a successful song or performance

(i) a cheap person

(j) foolish or playful behavior

ANSWERS ARE ON PAGE 298.

EXERCISE 6

Directions: Write *L* if the statement is literal or *F* if it is figurative.

_____ **1.** On July 20, 1969, two men walked on the moon.

_____ **2.** The prizefighter kissed the canvas.

_____ **3.** I've got the blues.

_____ **4.** The lion tamer cracked his whip.

_____ **5.** A dentist was the first patient to receive an artificial heart.

_____ **6.** The horror movie was a hair-raising experience.

_____ **7.** He soft-soaped his boss.

_____ **8.** The actor Clark Gable was a lady-killer.

_____ **9.** The fire fighters rescued the children from the burning building.

_____ **10.** The fly was trapped in the spider web.

ANSWERS ARE ON PAGE 298.

FIGURATIVE LANGUAGE IN LITERATURE

Through figurative language, authors invent original ways of describing a subject or expressing emotions. You can experience how authors see and interpret the world by understanding their figurative language.

The figurative language used in poetry, fiction, and drama is more moving than the literal language used in newspaper articles. For example, a part of the weather forecast might say, "mostly cloudy, overcast skies." This is a factual report, stated directly.

In William Shakespeare's play *Romeo and Juliet,* a tragic love story, the playwright describes the same weather conditions in figurative language. After Romeo and Juliet have died, Shakespeare writes at the end of the play:

The sun, for sorrow, will not show its head.

Shakespeare gives the sun human qualities. The sun is unhappy and appears to be mourning the death of Romeo and Juliet. Because of its grief, "the sun will not show its head," or, in other words, will not appear in the sky. What can you infer from Shakespeare's description?

The sky is dark and overcast, and the atmosphere is gloomy.

Of course, Shakespeare never told you directly. You interpreted the meaning from the figurative language. Compare Shakespeare's description to the newspaper account of the weather presented earlier. Shakespeare's words create an imaginary picture and express strong feelings. In contrast, you probably did not respond emotionally to the literal statement about the sky.

Look at how another author, John McPhee, uses figurative language. In the following excerpt, he describes a basketball player:

> A star is often a point-hungry gunner, whose first instinct when he gets the ball is to fire away, and whose playing creed might be condensed to "When in doubt, shoot." Another, with legs like automobile springs, is part of the group because of an unusual ability to go high for rebounds.
>
> —Excerpted from *A Sense of Where You Are*

In his description, McPhee makes two comparisons:

1. "A *star* is often a point-hungry *gunner*, whose first instinct when he gets the ball is to fire away"

2. "*legs* like *automobile springs*"

What do these comparisons show? The first presents an exaggerated image of a star player by comparing how he instinctively shoots baskets to how a gunner instinctively shoots at targets. The second emphasizes the rebounding power of a basketball player's legs.

Here are some suggestions for interpreting figurative language:

- Identify the comparisons—direct or implied.

- Picture in your mind the two images being compared; for example, a basketball player's legs and automobile springs.

- Determine the author's purpose in drawing the comparison. What is the author trying to show you?

EXERCISE 7

Directions: For each excerpt, identify the two things being compared. Then interpret why the author has made the comparison. Follow the example below.

> My father is eighty-six years old and in bed. His heart, that bloody motor, is equally old and will not do certain jobs any more. It still floods his head with brainy light. But it won't let his legs carry the weight of his body around the house.
>
> —Excerpted from "A Conversation with My Father" by Grace Paley

The father's heart is compared to *an old motor*.

Interpretation (why the author has made the comparison): *The comparison explains why the father's heart condition has confined him to his bed.*

1. "Earlier in the evening it had rained, and now icicles hung along the station-house eaves like some crystal monster's vicious teeth."

   —Excerpted from "A Tree of Night" by Truman Capote

   _____ is compared to _____.

   Interpretation: _____

   _____

2. "I feel as if I were walking a tight-rope a hundred feet over a circus audience and suddenly the rope is showing signs of breaking. . . ."

   —Excerpted from *In Dreams Begin Responsibilities* by Delmore Schwartz

   _____ is compared to _____.

   Interpretation: _____

   _____

3. "The lid of the left eye twitched; it fell down and snapped up; it was exactly as though the lid of the eye were a window shade and someone stood inside the doctor's head playing with the cord."

—Excerpted from *Winesburg, Ohio* by Sherwood Anderson

_____ is compared to _____.

Interpretation: _____

_____

4. "The heavy noon-day sun hit him directly in the face, beating down on him like a club."

—Excerpted from *The Day of the Locust* by Nathanael West

_____ is compared to _____.

Interpretation: _____

_____

5. "Lucy wiped the perspiration-soaked wisp of hair back from her face, and gave that last-minute look around the table to see if anything was missing, like a general inspecting troops."

—Excerpted from *All the King's Men* by Robert Penn Warren

_____ is compared to _____.

Interpretation: _____

_____

6. "The high grey-flannel fog of winter closed off Salinas Valley from the sky and from the rest of the world."

—Excerpted from "The Chrysanthemums" by John Steinbeck

_____ is compared to _____.

Interpretation: _____

_____

ANSWERS ARE ON PAGE 299.

APPLICATION

On the GED Literature and the Arts Test, you will be asked to transfer your understanding of a concept that you learned about in a passage to a different situation. This reading skill, called **_application_**, requires two steps:

1. First, you must thoroughly understand the main idea or supporting details of a passage.

2. Second, you must apply this information to a new context or setting.

Use this approach as you read the following paragraph:

> When you interview for a job, you want to make a good first impression. Dressing neatly and professionally shows the interviewer that you take pride in your appearance. Therefore, use good judgment in selecting the clothes you wear on a job interview. Don't wear outfits that are too casual or flashy.

Suppose you were interviewing for an office job at a local business. Which of the following clothes should you choose to wear for the interview?

(1) a suit
(2) blue jeans and a sweater
(3) formal evening wear

The answer is (1). You applied the advice on how to dress in the appropriate way for a job interview to a new situation. A suit is neat and professional. Blue jeans and a sweater are too casual, and formal evening wear is too dressy.

Another way of applying ideas is to see a concept or a situation in a different historical context. For example, Shakespeare's play _Romeo and Juliet_, written in the sixteenth century, takes place in an Italian city. The story is about two feuding families—the Montagues and the Capulets. Romeo and Juliet, who are on opposite sides of the feud, fall in love with each other. Despite their families' disapproval, they secretly marry. However, Romeo and Juliet's love is not strong enough to overcome the hatred between their families. Their relationship is doomed to end tragically.

The musical _West Side Story_ applies the story of Romeo and Juliet to a modern-day situation. The story takes place in New York City. Instead of feuding families, _West Side Story_ is about two feuding gangs of teenagers—the Sharks and the Jets. Like Romeo and Juliet, Tony and Maria fall in love, although each associates with a rival gang. Caught in the middle of the conflict, they, too, face tragedy in the end.

EXERCISE 8

Directions: Read the passage below and answer the questions that follow.

Vocational schools can offer sound training for young people who are not college bound and for adults interested in changing or expanding their technical or service training.

Education should be purchased as carefully as any other services, and the source of any course of study should be carefully investigated before you invest in it.

Whether it is a course in automobile mechanics, drafting, practical nursing, locksmithing, or any of the range of vocational education areas that interest you, **move carefully**. Find out whether the course you want is available from the public school system—many vocational courses are. Tuition may be minimal and the quality of instruction excellent, and courses may be offered in night school or adult education classes so that students are able to work during the day and continue their education simultaneously.

Check with your high school guidance counselor for information on public vocational schools.

Do your homework **before** you sign up with any private vocational schools. Get answers to these questions:

- Find out how many students were admitted to the school, and how many actually graduated.

- Ask for names and addresses of students who graduated in the past six months. Give them a call.

- Is the school licensed by the state? Call [your state's] Department of Education.

- Is the school accredited by an agency recognized by the U.S. Office of Education, or the Council on Postsecondary Accreditation? (Don't assume that accreditation means that the school is good.)

- If you sign an installment contract for payment for the course, who holds the collection contract? Sometimes your contract is sold to a bank or a finance company, which means that if you have questions about the financial arrangements, you may have to deal with a company other than the school.

Move slowly. There is always another time, and another semester. Reputable schools have no reason to use high-pressure salespeople to solicit students. If the school representative says you must sign a contract (which may be labeled **Application for Enrollment** or **Enrollment Agreement**) to reserve your place in next semester's class—forget it. A reputable school will give you time to check its credentials.

—Excerpted from the *Consumer Resource Book* by the Better
Business Bureau of Chicago and Northern Illinois, Inc.

Answer the questions below by circling *yes* or *no*. If the situation is an application of the advice given in the passage, choose *yes*. If it contradicts the advice, choose *no*.

1. An educational counselor from a trade school tells an applicant, "We place 98 percent of our graduates in top-paying jobs. They all have rewarding careers with the most successful companies in the city."

   yes   no   Should the applicant assume that the counselor is telling the truth?

2. At High-Tech, Inc., a computer training school, Maria takes a mathematical aptitude exam. According to the school's admissions representative, Maria's remarkably high test score indicates that she has the potential to become a computer programmer with an annual salary of $50,000.

   yes   no   Should Maria believe that this test accurately measures her ability and predicts her possible yearly income?

3. Sam telephones the personnel director of Worldwide Cartage, which has a good reputation. He asks if the company hires graduates from Randolph Trucking School. She replies, "Yes. We try to staff our positions with graduates of Randolph. Overall, they make excellent employees."

   yes   no   Based on the personnel director's recommendation, should Sam consider attending Randolph Trucking School?

4. Felicia wants to become a lab technician. A friend of hers, Sandra, attended Medical Careers Institute and dropped out. When Felicia asked Sandra why, Sandra replied, "The teachers give too much homework. I didn't have enough time to spend with my kids."

   yes   no   Does Felicia have enough information to judge the quality of education at Medical Careers Institute?

5. On a TV commercial, a well-dressed young man says that he graduated from Alexander Technical College. He shows the new stereo and car he just bought because he landed such a great job. He thanks the technical college for his current success.

   yes   no   Should you assume that any graduate from Alexander Technical College could tell a similar success story?

6. Cindy has just completed her first interview with the Franklin School of Commerce. The interviewer told her, "Our enrollment in the accounting program is limited to fifty students. If I were you, I'd sign the Enrollment Agreement right now. We have room for only four more students. By tomorrow, we'll probably have no openings."

   yes   no   Should Cindy postpone signing the Enrollment Agreement?

ANSWERS ARE ON PAGE 299.

INFERENTIAL UNDERSTANDING

Read each passage below and choose the best answer to each question that follows.

Questions 1–6 refer to the following excerpt from an essay.

WHAT KIND OF PEOPLE ARE THESE CONSTRUCTION WORKERS?

They drive into town in big cars, and live in furnished rooms, and drink whiskey with beer chasers, and chase women they will soon forget. They linger only a little while,
5 only until they have built the bridge; then they are off again to another town, another bridge, linking everything but their lives.

They possess none of the foundation of their bridges. They are part circus, part
10 gypsy—graceful in the air, restless on the ground; it is as if the wide-open road below lacks for them the clear direction of an eight-inch beam stretching across the sky six hundred feet above the sea.

15 When there are no bridges to be built, they will build skyscrapers, or highways, or power dams, or anything that promises a challenge—and overtime. They will go anywhere, will drive a thousand miles all day
20 and night to be part of a new building boom. They find boom towns irresistible. That is why they are called "the boomers."

In appearance, boomers usually are big men, or if not always big, always strong, and
25 their skin is ruddy from all the sun and wind. Some who heat rivets have charred complexions; some who drive rivets are hard of hearing; some who catch rivets in small metal cones have blisters and body burns
30 marking each miss; some who do welding see flashes at night while they sleep. Those who connect steel have deep scars along their shins from climbing columns. Many boomers have mangled hands and fingers
35 sliced off by slipped steel. Most have taken falls and broken a limb or two. All have seen death.

They are cocky men, men of great pride, and at night they brag and build bridges in
40 bars, and sometimes when they are turning to leave, the bartender will yell after them, "Hey, you guys, how's about clearing some steel out of here?"

—Gay Talese, excerpted from "The Bridge," 1964

1. The purpose of this passage is to

   (1) explain why construction work is a rewarding career
   (2) describe the physical appearance of construction workers
   (3) illustrate how skyscrapers and bridges are built
   (4) suggest that construction workers are irresponsible
   (5) show the personalities of construction workers

2. Why does the author use the phrase "part circus, part gypsy" (lines 9–10)? To

   (1) explain why construction workers like to travel
   (2) show how construction workers are similar to acrobats and roaming people
   (3) contrast the differences between construction workers and entertainers
   (4) show that construction workers are men of great pride
   (5) illustrate construction workers' outdoor activities

3. The construction workers are called *the boomers* because

   (1) they are attracted to new building developments
   (2) they have loud and boisterous personalities
   (3) their rivets make an exploding sound
   (4) they earn extra money working overtime
   (5) their voices sound like thunder

4. Which statement best expresses the main idea of the fourth paragraph?

   (1) Welders and riveters are careless workers.
   (2) Construction workers have strong muscles.
   (3) Construction work is a dangerous job.
   (4) Construction work requires special skills.
   (5) Construction workers fear injuries and death.

5. You can infer from this excerpt that construction workers would be least likely to

   (1) flirt with women they hardly know
   (2) settle down and lead a safe, easygoing life
   (3) perform other kinds of physical labor
   (4) party wildly with friends at a bar
   (5) seek out adventures and thrilling situations

6. If the construction workers had lived in the late nineteenth century, they would probably have

   (1) built railroads
   (2) raised cattle
   (3) planted crops
   (4) sold real estate
   (5) served liquor

Questions 7–12 refer to the following excerpt from a short story.

WHO IS CONNIE?

Her name was Connie. She was fifteen and had a quick nervous giggling habit of craning her neck to glance into mirrors, or checking other people's faces to make sure
5　her own was all right. Her mother, who noticed everything and knew everything and who hadn't much reason any longer to look at her own face, always scolded Connie about it. "Stop gawking at yourself, who are
10　you? You think you're so pretty?" she would say. Connie would raise her eyebrows at these familiar complaints and look right through her mother, into a shadowy vision of herself as she was right at that moment: she
15　knew she was pretty and that was everything. Her mother had been pretty once too, if you could believe those old snapshots in the album, but now her looks were gone and that was why she was always
20　after Connie.

"Why don't you keep your room clean like your sister? How've you got your hair fixed—what the hell stinks? Hair spray? You don't see your sister using that junk."

25　Her sister June was twenty-four and still lived at home. She was a secretary in the high school Connie attended, and if that wasn't bad enough—with her in the same building—she was so plain and chunky and
30　steady that Connie had to hear her praised all the time by her mother and her mother's sisters. June did this, June did that, she saved money and helped clean the house and cooked and Connie couldn't do a thing,
35　her mind was filled with trashy daydreams. Their father was away at work most of the time and when he came home he wanted supper and he read the newspaper at supper and after supper he went to bed.

—Joyce Carol Oates, excerpted from "Where Are You Going, Where Have You Been?" 1970

7. How does the mother feel about Connie?

　(1) jealous
　(2) embarrassed
　(3) admiring
　(4) sympathetic
　(5) concerned

8. ". . . she knew she was pretty and that was everything . . ." (lines 14–16). The author includes this description to show that Connie

　(1) wants to be a fashion model
　(2) needs to attract teenage boys
　(3) is conceited about her looks
　(4) plans to enter a beauty contest
　(5) fears her beauty will fade

9. Which of the following statements best describes the mother's opinion of June?

　(1) June should get married.
　(2) June should lose weight.
　(3) June is kinder than Connie.
　(4) June is a capable secretary.
　(5) June is her favorite daughter.

10. Why does the author use the phrase "trashy daydreams" (line 35)? To

　(1) compare Connie's daydreams to her messy room
　(2) contrast Connie's mind with a garbage can
　(3) imply that the mother doesn't have those kinds of daydreams
　(4) suggest that Connie's mother thinks Connie's inner thoughts are worthless
　(5) explain why Connie doesn't enjoy housework

11. From the description of the father (lines 36–39), you can conclude that he

　(1) is irritable from working long hours
　(2) does not spend much time with his family
　(3) takes pride in supporting his family
　(4) likes to read about current events
　(5) enjoys being with his wife and daughters

12. In this passage, Connie's family is described by a fiction writer. Connie's home life could also be analyzed from the point of view of a

　(1) housekeeper
　(2) family counselor
　(3) hairstylist
　(4) scientist
　(5) historian

Questions 13–17 refer to the following excerpt from an essay.

WHAT DOES A WRITER EXPERIENCE?

Having, from a conversation overheard or in some other way, got the tone of a tale, I was like a woman who has just become impregnated. Something was growing inside
5   me. At night when I lay in bed I could feel the heels of the tale kicking against the walls of my body. Often as I lay thus every word of the tale came to me quite clearly but when I got out of bed to write it down the
10 words would not come.

I had constantly to seek in roads new to me. Other men had felt what I had felt, had seen what I had seen—how had they met the difficulties I faced? My father when he
15 told his tales walked up and down the room before his audience. He pushed out little experimental sentences and watched his audience narrowly. There was a dull-eyed old farmer sitting in a corner of the room.
20 Father had his eyes on the fellow. "I'll get him," he said to himself. He watched the farmer's eyes. When the experimental sentence he had tried did not get anywhere he tried another and kept trying. Beside
25 words he had—to help the telling of his tales—the advantage of being able to act out those parts for which he could find no words. He could frown, shake his fists, smile, let a look of pain or annoyance drift over
30 his face.

These were his advantages that I had to give up if I was to write my tales rather than tell them and how often I had cursed my fate.

—Sherwood Anderson, excerpted from "On Form, Not Plot, in the Short Story," 1924

13. In lines 1–7, why does the author compare himself to a pregnant woman? To

   (1) show sympathy for women writers
   (2) illustrate that writers carry heavy burdens
   (3) show that a story "grows" inside him
   (4) imply that he has a large belly
   (5) show respect for mothers and infants

14. What statement best summarizes the main idea of the second paragraph?

   (1) The farmers didn't enjoy listening to the stories of the author's father.
   (2) The author's father could use gestures as well as words to capture his audience's attention.
   (3) The author's father experimented with his sentences.
   (4) The author faced many hardships during his lifetime.
   (5) The author's father should have become a professional actor.

15. Which of the following words best describes the author's feelings toward his father?

   (1) respect
   (2) resentment
   (3) boredom
   (4) shame
   (5) sympathy

16. From the final sentence, what can you conclude about the author's attitude toward writing?

   (1) He would rather write speeches than stories.
   (2) He frequently struggles over his decision to become a writer.
   (3) He regards writing as predictable and routine.
   (4) Writing offers little personal satisfaction.
   (5) He believes that writing a story has more advantages than telling it.

17. Which of the following people would most closely identify with the author's occupation?

   (1) a baby doctor
   (2) a farmer
   (3) a typist
   (4) an artist
   (5) a stagehand

ANSWERS ARE ON PAGE 299.

Popular singer Julio Iglesias has a style all his own. Authors also may have distinctive styles.

If you listen to the morning news on the radio, you have heard the daily traffic report. A newscaster, flying over the city in a helicopter, might say:

> Rush hour traffic is stop and go on all major expressways. Roads are slick from last night's storm. An overturned truck on Highway 42 has caused delays. Motorists are advised to take an alternate route. Travel time from the western suburbs to downtown is about forty-five minutes.

Notice that the reporter examines certain elements, such as accidents, traffic patterns, weather, and road conditions. The traffic reporter is using the reasoning process called *analysis*. She breaks down a situation into its basic parts, then shows how each relates to the total picture—an overview of traffic.

Similarly, handwriting experts analyze personality traits as revealed by an individual's penmanship. They study the size and shape of the letters and pay close attention to particular strokes.

The illustration provides you with several examples of how handwriting experts analyze personality according to the way letters are formed.

h	A letter extending out to the right suggests warmth and a desire to reach out and communicate with others.
T	The heavy strokes in this letter indicate strength and force. This writer is energetic and determined to succeed.
m	The soft, rounded curves in this letter reveal an even temper and a desire to be agreeable to others.
F	The ornate flourishes in this letter indicate that the writer is overly concerned with appearance and may be somewhat vain.
n	The end stroke of this letter stretches upward as if toward heaven. This writer has high aspirations and is capable of deep spirituality.
Sue	This writer calls attention to herself by underlining her first name. She is confident and has a strong sense of accomplishment.

Did you notice that the explanation beside each letter is analytical? Certain characteristics of the letter are identified and then associated with specific personality traits—for example, warmth, spirituality, or confidence. By analyzing the basic components of a person's handwriting, the expert hopes to gain a better understanding of the person.

In the same way, you can gain a better understanding of a passage through the analytical thought process. By breaking a passage down into its basic parts and seeing how they relate to each other, you will have a better idea of *what* the passage means as well as *how* the writer conveyed the meaning. Seeing "the why" and "the how" will help you succeed on the GED Literature and the Arts Test.

In reading, analysis requires two steps:

1. identifying the elements of style and structure in the passage

2. determining how these elements create an overall effect

You use analysis in your everyday experiences. For instance, one important application of this skill is in looking for a new job. Before you begin planning your job search, you need to analyze who you are and what you want out of a job. More specifically, you need to think about the following things:

- your job skills and qualifications

- your work habits

- your likes and dislikes

- your career goals

The work sheet on the next page is designed to help you analyze these areas.

First, answer the questions on the work sheet and review your answers. If possible, discuss your answers with a family member, friend, or someone else who knows you well. This preliminary analysis should give you a better understanding of yourself and the type of job that would suit you. Then, if you want, write a brief summary of your self-evaluation. On another piece of paper, write a paragraph about your most outstanding job qualifications, a paragraph about your work habits and preferences, and a paragraph about your career goals.

SELF-EVALUATION WORK SHEET

The following are some of the things you should consider in your own self-evaluation. Your answers should be honest. They are meant to help you and should not represent a "good" or "bad" value judgment.

1. What are the things you do best? Are they related to people, data, things?

_____ related to _____
_____ related to _____
_____ related to _____

2. Do you express yourself well and easily?
Orally: ☐ Yes ☐ No   In writing: ☐ Yes ☐ No

3. Do you see yourself as a leader of a group or team? ☐ Yes ☐ No

Do you see yourself as an active participant of a group or team?
☐ Yes ☐ No

Do you prefer to work on your own? ☐ Yes ☐ No

Do you like supervision? ☐ Yes ☐ No

4. Do you work well under pressure? ☐ Yes ☐ No

Does pressure cause you anxiety; in fact, is it difficult for you to work well under pressure? ☐ Yes ☐ No

5. Do you seek responsibility? ☐ Yes ☐ No

Do you prefer to follow directions? ☐ Yes ☐ No

6. Do you enjoy new ideas and situations? ☐ Yes ☐ No

Are you more comfortable with known routines? ☐ Yes ☐ No

7. In your future, which of the following things are most important to you:
☐ **a.** Working for a regular salary
☐ **b.** Working for a commission
☐ **c.** Working for a combination of both

8. Do you want to work a regular schedule (e.g., 9 A.M. to 5 P.M.)?
☐ Yes ☐ No

9. Are you willing to travel more than 50 percent of your working time?
☐ Yes ☐ No

10. What kind of environment is important to you?
a. Do you prefer to work indoors? ☐ Yes ☐ No
b. Do you prefer to work outdoors? ☐ Yes ☐ No
c. Do you prefer an urban environment (population over a million)?
☐ Yes ☐ No
Population between 100,000 to 900,000? ☐ Yes ☐ No
d. Do you prefer a rural setting? ☐ Yes ☐ No

11. Do you prefer to work for a large organization? ☐ Yes ☐ No

12. Are you free to move? ☐ Yes ☐ No

Are there important "others" to be considered? ☐ Yes ☐ No

—From *Business Communications* by Michael E. Adelstein and W. Keats Sparrow

STYLE

You have probably heard the term *style* used in various contexts. For instance, clothing designers create styles of fashion—distinctive ways of dressing. Designers believe that people's choice of clothes makes a fashion statement—a comment about their personalities and background.

The term *style* can also be applied to literature and the arts. In this context, **style** refers to the distinguishing characteristics of an artist's performance and work—his or her unique way of singing or dancing or writing. For example, imagine how three very different singers might perform the same song. Contrast how "Happy Birthday" might sound as sung by Frank Sinatra, Michael Jackson, and Johnny Cash. Each would imprint his own way of singing on the song, and it would sound very different as performed by each.

Styles of writing vary as much as styles of fashion and musical performance. Because each author's personality and talents are unique, the style of a written passage is highly individual. How is this individuality achieved? The author's craft—his or her skills in expression through language—results in a distinctive style. In this section, you will learn to analyze two elements that affect an author's style:

- diction

- tone

DICTION

Before authors begin writing, they might ask themselves these questions:

- What is my purpose for writing? To persuade? To inform? To entertain?

- What is my topic?

- Who is my audience?

- What response do I want from my readers?

The answers to these questions affect the author's **diction**—the words used to express ideas. Diction, or word choice, characterizes an author's writing style.

The following paragraph illustrates different styles of diction. What do you observe about the ways that the scientist, the engineer, the foreman, and the salesman use language? As you read, notice that their statements are related to the function of levers.

> Note the many languages within our language. The college freshman learns that "the moment of force about any specified axis is the product of the force and perpendicular distance from the axis to the line of action of the force." Viewing the same physical principle, the engineer says: "To lift a heavy weight with a lever, a man should apply his strength to the end of a long lever arm and work the weight on a

short lever arm." Out on the factory floor the foreman shouts, "Shove that brick up snug under the crowbar and get a good purchase; the crate is heavy." The salesman says: "Why let your men kill themselves heaving those boxes all day long? The job's easy with this new long-handled pinch bar. With today's high wages you'll save the cost the first afternoon."

—Excerpted from "Giving Power to Words"
by Philip W. Swain

Examine these four statements and analyze the writing styles.

TYPES OF DICTION

Statement	Analysis
Scientist: "The moment of force about any specified axis is the product of the force and perpendicular distance from the axis to the line of action of the force."	This style is formal. The scientist explains how a lever works according to the principles of physics. She assumes her audience has a scientific background and can understand technical language.
Engineer: "To lift a heavy weight with a lever, a man should apply his strength to the end of a long lever arm and work the weight on a short lever arm."	This style is informal. The engineer uses simpler words to explain how to operate a lever. His message is geared toward a general audience.
Foreman: "Shove that brick up snug under the crowbar and get a good purchase; the crate is heavy."	This style is conversational. The foreman uses words and colorful expressions from everyday speech. The foreman does not scientifically explain that the crowbar is a lever. He directly tells another factory worker how to lift a crate with a crowbar.
Salesman: "Why let your men kill themselves heaving those boxes all day long? The job's easy with this new long-handled pinch bar. With today's high wages you'll save the cost the first afternoon."	This style is also conversational. The salesman's purpose, however, is to persuade factory managers to purchase his product—a crowbar.

You can analyze an author's diction as formal, informal, or conversational. A ***formal style*** is usually found in scholarly essays, legal documents, and technical articles. The reading level is often very challenging.

An ***informal style*** generally appears in magazine and newspaper articles. The author's choice of words is directed to the general reading public.

A ***conversational style*** imitates the way people speak. It may include slang expressions such as *nerd* and *gross*.

Fiction writers may choose to tell an entire story in one of these three styles. However, sometimes they combine different kinds of diction. For example, they might write a character description in an informal style and a character's dialogue in a conversational style.

Notice the different language used in each of the following statements:

Formal: Two officers arrested Mr. Bowman, the motorist, for driving his automobile under the influence of alcohol. His blood alcohol content (BAC), the percentage of alcohol in his blood, was higher than .10.

Informal: Two officers arrested Mr. Bowman for drunken driving.

Conversational: Two cops threw Bowman into the slammer for driving his car while he was smashed on booze.

EXERCISE 1

Directions: What kinds of writing styles—formal, informal, or conversational—would you probably find in each of the following examples? Fill in the blank for each.

1. A letter to a close friend _____

2. A TV commercial starring football players drinking beer _____

3. A doctor's medical report analyzing childhood diseases _____

4. A brochure for parents on taking care of a newborn baby _____

5. A lawyer's movie contract for a film star _____

6. A newspaper article on drug abuse in professional sports _____

7. An advice column written by Ann Landers _____

8. A magazine article about Disneyland _____

ANSWERS ARE ON PAGE 300.

EXERCISE 2

Directions: Identify the style of each excerpt as *formal*, *informal*, or *conversational*.

1. "It was Paul's afternoon to appear before the faculty of the Pittsburgh High School to account for his various misdemeanors. He had been suspended a week ago, and his father had called at the Principal's office and confessed his perplexity about his son. Paul entered the faculty room suave and smiling."

—Excerpted from "Paul's Case" by Willa Cather

Style ————————————————

2. "You see that cat inside the bar with that long fingernail, don't you? Well, he uses that nail to mark cards with. Every time I get in a game, there is somebody dealing with a long fingernail. It ain't safe!"

—Excerpted from "Conversation on the Corner" by Langston Hughes

Style ————————————————

3. "Few evils are less accessible to the force of reason, or more tenacious of life and power, than long-standing prejudice. It is a moral disorder, which creates the conditions necessary to its own existence, and fortifies itself by refusing all contradiction. It paints a hateful picture according to its own diseased imagination, and distorts the features of the fancied original to suit the portrait."

—Excerpted from "The Color Line" by Frederick Douglass

Style ————————————————

4. "Jack is wandering around town, not knowing what to do. His girlfriend is babysitting at the Tuckers', and later, when she's got the kids in bed, maybe he'll drop over there. Sometimes he watches TV with her when she's babysitting, it's about the only chance he gets to make out a little since he doesn't own wheels, but they have to be careful because most people don't like their sitters to have their boyfriends over."

—Excerpted from "The Babysitter" by Robert Coover

Style ————————————————

5. "The saloon is the most important building in the Western. It is the only place in the story where people can be seen together time after time. It thereby functions as a meetinghouse, social center, church. More important, it is the setting for the climax of the story, the gunfight. No matter where the fight ends, it starts in the saloon."

—Excerpted from "The Western: The Legend and the Cardboard Hero" by Peter Homans

Style ————————————————

ANSWERS ARE ON PAGE 300.

Figurative Language and Style

In Chapter 2, you learned that figures of speech often make direct or implied comparisons between two things. Figurative language suggests a meaning beyond the literal definition of the words.

When you are analyzing the diction of a passage, you should notice if the author uses figurative language. Figurative language characterizes some authors' styles. Through figures of speech, an author can more vividly convey his or her feelings or viewpoints.

For example, Octavio Paz, the 1990 Nobel Prize winner for literature, sometimes uses figurative language and images to communicate his beliefs. His speech "In Search of the Present" uses an imaginative style to illustrate abstract concepts.

> The consciousness of being separate is a constant feature of our spiritual history. This separation is sometimes experienced as a wound that marks an internal division, an anguished awareness that invites introspection; at other times it appears as a challenge,
> 5 a spur to action, to go forth into the outside world and encounter others. It is true that the feeling of separation is universal and not peculiar to Spanish Americans. It is born at the very moment of our birth: as we are wrenched from the Whole, we fall into a foreign land. This never-healing wound is the unfathomable depth
> 10 of every man. All our ventures and exploits, all our acts and dreams, are bridges designed to overcome the separation and reunite us with the world and our fellow beings. Each man's life and the collective history of humanity can thus be seen as an attempt to reconstruct the original situation. An unfinished and
> 15 endless cure for our divided condition.

In this excerpt, Paz makes two comparisons:

- The feeling of being separate is like a wound (line 9).
- People's actions and dreams are like bridges designed to overcome the feelings of being separate from the world and "our fellow beings" (lines 10–12).

Why does Paz make these comparisons? The first comparison helps readers understand the feelings of separation experienced by some Spanish Americans. The author makes it easier for readers to relate to the loneliness by comparing it to something familiar to everyone—a wound. The second comparison helps readers understand how actions and dreams can overcome the feelings of separation and connect people with one another. Paz helps readers picture the abstract idea of connectedness by comparing it to a familiar object—a bridge.

≡ GED Practice ≡
EXERCISE 3

Read the excerpt from Paz's speech "In Search of the Present" and choose the best answer to each question that follows.

HOW DID THE AUTHOR FEEL AS A CHILD?

The feeling of separation is bound up
with the oldest and vaguest of my memories:
the first cry, the first scare. Like every child,
I built emotional bridges in the imagination
5 to link me to the world and to other people.
I lived in a town on the outskirts of Mexico
City, in an old dilapidated house that had a
junglelike garden and a great room full of
books. First games and first lessons. The
10 garden soon became the center of my
world; the library, an enchanted cave. I read
alone but played with my cousins and
schoolmates. There was a fig tree, temple of
vegetation, four pine trees, three ash trees, a
15 nightshade, a pomegranate tree, wild grass,
and prickly plants that produced purple
grazes. Adobe walls. Time was elastic; space
was a spinning wheel. All time, past or
future, real or imaginary, was pure presence,
20 and space transformed itself ceaselessly.
The beyond was here, all was here: a valley,
a mountain, a distant country, the neighbors'
patio. Books with pictures, especially history
books, eagerly leafed through, supplied
25 images of deserts and jungles, palaces and
hovels, warriors and princesses, beggars
and kings.

1. Paz's purpose in this passage about his childhood is to describe how

(1) poor his family was when he was growing up

(2) beautiful his family's garden was years ago

(3) he and his family traveled together to the mountains

(4) he used his imagination to link up with the world outside

(5) he taught himself all about the beauty of nature

2. What does Paz mean by the phrase "time was elastic" (line 17)?

(1) His imagination let him stretch time backward into the past or forward into the future.

(2) He had so much free time that he didn't know what to do with it.

(3) He had so few responsibilities that he could fill his time however he wished.

(4) His parents' library had so many books that he didn't have time to read them all.

(5) His picture books had many stories of times in the distant past.

3. At the center of Paz's childhood world was the

(1) garden
(2) city
(3) mountain range
(4) neighbors' patio
(5) library

ANSWERS ARE ON PAGE 300.

TONE

You have probably heard the expression *tone of voice*. If you tell a friend "I don't like your tone of voice," you are annoyed by the person's manner of speaking. You are reacting to the sound of the spoken words.

In your daily conversations, you make inferences about people's attitudes based on their speech—what they say and how they say it.

Imagine that you are observing the following situation. A customer in a restaurant is dissatisfied with his meal. The steak he ordered is too tough to eat. The way he phrases his complaint and the manner in which he says it to the waiter reveal his attitude. How would you describe the tone of each of these remarks?

1. "Would you please return the steak to the kitchen? Tell the chef that this cut of beef is a little too tough to eat."

2. "I refuse to pay for this steak dinner! How do you expect me to eat food that I can't chew? Let me see the restaurant manager. Now!"

3. "What animal did this steak come from? Only a power saw could cut through this meat!"

The first statement sounds courteous. The word *please* shows politeness.

The second statement reveals the customer's anger. He refuses to pay for his meal and demands to see the restaurant manager.

The third statement is sarcastic. By making a nasty joke about the food, the customer indirectly conveys his feelings. He does not expect the waiter to interpret the words literally.

A person's tone of voice may be described in several ways. Below are some examples. Add some of your own examples in the spaces provided.

friendly	phony	serious
sincere	sad	happy
understanding	polite	violent

_____   _____   _____

_____   _____   _____

WRITING ACTIVITY 1

Listen to a TV show or recall a recent conversation with a friend. Pay close attention to the person's tone of voice. On a separate sheet of paper, record three statements that you heard and indicate the attitude conveyed by the person's tone of voice.

ANSWERS WILL VARY.

Tone and Writing Style

Like tone of voice in speech, tone in writing expresses an attitude. In the study of literature, **_tone_** refers to an author's attitude toward his or her subject. The author's tone affects the way you respond to the author's subject.

When analyzing a passage for tone, ask yourself these questions:

- What subject is the author discussing?

- After reading the passage, what is my overall reaction?

- How does the author feel about the subject?

- What language or descriptive details reveal the author's attitude?

Answer these questions as you read the following excerpt from a newspaper column by Tom Bodett:

> Machinery and I have an understanding: we hate each other. I just have a hard time when it comes to fixing things. This, along with my inability to spit very far, is the most disappointing aspect of my life as a man. I do have some mechanical inclination. It's an attribute of my gender. There's a certain amount of knowledge about things mechanical that is passed on genetically from man to boy. Even my little son, when presented with a toy tractor, knew that blowing air through his flapping lips is what a tractor sounds like. He'd never seen a tractor until that day, but innately knew as much about them as I do. When tractors don't sound like flapping lips, they're broken. Of course, knowing when something is broken and knowing how to fix it are two separate fruits altogether.
>
> It is something of a tribal custom among the males of our species to hold forth on what we know about twirly things with gears and springs. If you want to entertain the menfolk on a slow Sunday, throw a broken lawnmower at their feet.
>
> "Must be the spark. She ain't gettin' no spark."
>
> "No, it ain't got fuel. Look, the plug's bone-dry."
>
> "Gotta be a stuck valve, you can feel there's no compression."
>
> "No spark, no fuel, no compression. That 'bout covers it. What do ya figure, Bubba?"
>
> "This is one broke lawnmower."
>
> —Excerpted from "Mechanical Inclinations"

The author's topic is men and machines. As you read the passage, you may have smiled or laughed at the author's attitude toward the topic. He pokes fun at the notion that men have an inborn ability to repair machines. How can you tell that the article is not to be taken seriously? Write your ideas on the line below.

_____

The opening sentence sets the tone for the rest of the article. The idea that a man has an agreement with machines is not to be taken seriously. Many other details tell you that the article is humorous: the author's overstatement about his inability to spit, the idea that tractors are broken if they don't sound like the air flapping through lips, and Bubba's final statement: "This is one broke lawnmower."

GED Practice
EXERCISE 4

For each excerpt, choose the best description of tone.

WHAT IS THE SPEAKER'S TONE?

1. "I am the whistler. And I know many things, for I walk by night. I know many strange tales hidden in the hearts of men and women who have stepped in the shadows. Yes . . . I know the nameless terrors of which they dare not speak."

   —Excerpted from the radio show "The Shadow"

   (1) threatening
   (2) silly
   (3) joyful
   (4) rude
   (5) encouraging

WHAT IS THE SPEAKER'S TONE?

2. "Fifteen. What a weird age to be male. Most of us have forgotten about it, or have idealized it. But when you are fifteen . . . well, things tend to be less than perfect.

   "You can't drive. You are only a freshman in high school. The girls your age look older than you and go out with upperclassmen who have cars. You probably don't shave. You have nothing to do on weekends."

   —Bob Greene, excerpted from "Fifteen," 1982

   (1) serious
   (2) nasty
   (3) funny
   (4) grim
   (5) angry

WHAT IS THE SPEAKER'S TONE?

3. "About five o'clock our procession of three cars reached the cemetery and stopped in a thick drizzle beside the gate—first a motor hearse, horribly black and wet, then Mr. Gatz and the minister and I in the limousine, and a little later four or five servants and the postman from West Egg, in Gatsby's station wagon, all wet to the skin."

   —F. Scott Fitzgerald, excerpted from *The Great Gatsby*, 1925

   (1) somber
   (2) disrespectful
   (3) insincere
   (4) peaceful
   (5) happy

WHAT IS THE SPEAKER'S TONE?

4. These devils will afflict the damned in two ways, by their presence and by their reproaches. We can have no idea how horrible these devils are. Saint Catherine of Siena once saw a devil and she has written that, rather than look again for one single instant on such a frightful monster, she would prefer to walk until the end of her life along a track of red coals.

   —James Joyce, excerpted from *A Portrait of the Artist as a Young Man*, 1916

   (1) sarcastic
   (2) mysterious
   (3) friendly
   (4) intimidating
   (5) gentle

ANSWERS ARE ON PAGE 300.

EXERCISE 3

Directions: Read the passage below and answer the questions that follow.

WHAT MAKES A MANAGER GOOD?

Every few years business leaders celebrate the birth of "new" management techniques and new gimmicks that promise to solve employee, customer and product quality problems. It's as if new were synonymous with better. Well, it isn't.

Management By Walking Around (MBWA), one of the newer techniques, is nothing more than caring enough about what's going on in the organization to talk to the people who know. Nothing new there. And, Total Quality Management (TQM), still another "new" technique, is a matter of instilling old-fashioned pride.

While new management techniques may look different from those they are supposed to replace, they don't qualify as a better means of accomplishing the results corporate executives are paid to produce. New techniques do not improve morale, productivity, quality or profits. At best, they offer short-lived hope and excitement, which any changes, even superficial ones, usually engender. They also generate a new vocabulary, buzzwords—which seem to give techniques legitimacy—and structured programs designed to implement the techniques.

Experience shows that technique-oriented programs eventually die, but not because the techniques themselves are bad. The problem is that many users are not true believers of the emotional and intellectual assumptions the techniques reflect.

Suppose, for example, a manager learns how to use the techniques of Management By Objectives, but really believes that the only objectives that count are the manager's. MBO is doomed to fail.

Many managers employ techniques that do not represent their basic values or true feelings. Yet, they go through the motions because they would like to think that the techniques they've learned have powers— independent of anything else—to accomplish results. The fact is, techniques for managing people that do not come from the soul—from emotions—from a genuine caring attitude, come across as phony and artificial. Unless managers' people-managing techniques are extensions of their values and beliefs, they will, almost invariably, revert to their natural ways.

—Excerpted from "Techniques Do Not a Good Manager Make"
by Jack H. Grossman

1. Name two "new" management techniques that, according to the excerpt, are popular. Then briefly explain what each consists of.

2. What does the writer feel is most important in helping to solve employee problems?

ANSWERS ARE ON PAGE 301.

SPORTS AND ENTERTAINMENT

The next four excerpts address issues relating to how people spend their free time. The selections cover a variety of topics ranging from the disadvantages of glorifying athletics to the benefits of playing video games.

EXERCISE 4

Directions: Read the passage below and answer the questions that follow.

WHAT IS A PROFESSIONAL ATHLETE'S ATTITUDE TOWARD EDUCATION?

Somehow, parents must instill a desire for learning alongside the desire to be Walt Frazier. Why not start by sending black professional athletes into high schools to explain the facts of life?

5 I have often addressed high school audiences and my message is always the same: "For every hour you spend on the athletic field, spend two in the library. Even if you make it as a pro athlete, your career will be over by the time you are 35. You will need that diploma."

Have these pro athletes explain what happens if you break a leg, get a sore arm, have one bad year or don't make the cut for five or six
10 tournaments. Explain to them the star system, wherein for every star earning millions there are six or seven others making $15,000 or $20,000 or $30,000. Invite a bench-warmer or a guy who didn't make it. Ask him if he sleeps every night. Ask him whether he was graduated. Ask him what he would do if he became disabled tomorrow. Ask him where his old high
15 school athletic buddies are.

—Excerpted from "A Black Athlete Looks at Education" by Arthur Ashe

1. The most important message expressed in the passage is that

(1) parents should encourage their children to learn
(2) the careers of most professional athletes end at age thirty-five
(3) physical disabilities can ruin a professional athlete's career
(4) all aspiring athletes should realize the value of a high school diploma
(5) only a minority of professional athletes earn amazingly high salaries

2. If a statement supports the author's viewpoint, write *valid*. If the statement does not reflect the author's viewpoint, write *invalid*.

_____ **(1)** Most professional athletes are stupid.

_____ **(2)** Many high school students are shortsighted about the realities of professional sports.

_____ **(3)** Many high school athletes underestimate the importance of education.

_____ **(4)** Athletic superstars are paid too much money.

_____ **(5)** Some professional athletes don't sleep at night because they are studying.

ANSWERS ARE ON PAGE 301.

GED Practice
EXERCISE 5

Read the passage below and choose the best answer to each question that follows.

WHY IS FELIPE BEING FOLLOWED?

White men in suits follow Felipe Lopez
everywhere he goes. Felipe lives in Mott
Haven, in the South Bronx. He is a junior at
Rice High School, which is on the corner of
5 124th Street and Lenox Avenue, in Harlem,
and he plays guard for the school basketball
team, the Rice Raiders. The white men are
ubiquitous. They rarely miss one of Felipe's
games or tournaments. They have absolute
10 recall of his best minutes of play. They are
authorities on his physical condition. They
admire his feet, which are big and pontoon-
shaped, and his wrists, which have a loose,
silky motion. Not long ago, I sat with the
15 white men at a game between Rice and All
Hallows High School. My halftime
entertainment was listening to a debate
between two of them—a college scout and a
Westchester contractor who is a high-school
20 basketball fan—about whether Felipe had
grown a half inch over Christmas break. "I
know this kid," the scout said as the second
half started. "A half inch is not something I
would miss." The white men believe that
25 Felipe is the best high-school basketball
player in the country. They often compare
him to Michael Jordan, and are betting he
will become one of the greatest basketball
players to emerge from New York City since
30 Kareem Abdul-Jabbar. This conjecture
provides them with suspended, savory
excitement and a happy premonition.
Following Felipe is like hanging around with
someone you think is going to win the
35 lottery someday.

—Susan Orlean, excerpted from "Shoot the
Moon," *The New Yorker*, March 22, 1993

1. Which statement best summarizes what this
excerpt is mainly about?

   (1) Government agents follow Felipe because
   they think he may be involved in illegal
   betting.
   (2) Boys who grow up and go to school in
   Harlem can become great basketball
   players.
   (3) The white men who follow Felipe know the
   scores for all his tournaments.
   (4) Many fans and scouts pay attention to
   Felipe because they believe he'll be a star
   player.
   (5) White men in suits are scouting around to
   find the best basketball player in the
   country.

2. In lines 7–8, when the writer states "The white
men are ubiquitous," she means they are

   (1) suspicious
   (2) everywhere
   (3) rich
   (4) friends
   (5) hiding

3. Why does the writer say, "Following Felipe is
like hanging around with someone you think is
going to win the lottery someday" (lines 33–
35)?

   (1) People are eager to associate with
   someone who they believe will become a
   winner.
   (2) People expect Felipe to be very generous
   when he gets rich.
   (3) The fans think Michael Jordan may show
   up at one of Felipe's basketball games.
   (4) The scouts need to make sure they don't
   miss a single game.
   (5) People are buying lottery tickets as gifts
   for Felipe.

ANSWERS ARE ON PAGE 301.

GED Practice
EXERCISE 6

Read the passage below and choose the best answer to each question that follows.

SHOULD CHILDREN PLAY VIDEO GAMES?

By many accounts, video games are a key element in getting children familiar with and used to an increasingly high-tech society. In 1983, *Psychology Today* reported
5 the results of a study in which kids had their "initiation into the world of computers by playing video games in the arcades or at home."

According to UCLA psychologist
10 Patricia Marks Greenfield, video games introduce them to the world of microcomputers at a time when computers are becoming increasingly important in many jobs and in daily life. In fact, many
15 computer programmers and technicians have gotten their first tastes of technology by playing such recreational devices.

Researchers continue to study their potential as educational tools. As MIT
20 researcher Sherry Turkel puts it, "There is nothing mindless about mastering a video game. [It] demands skills that are complex and differentiated . . . you interact with a program, you get used to assimilating large
25 amounts of information about structure and strategy by interacting with a dynamic screen display. And when one game is mastered, there is learning about how to generalize strategies to [others]. There is
30 learning how to learn."

Not all of the benefits of video game play stem from challenging graphics or a complex story-line. Some lie, instead, in the activity around the screen. The social
35 opportunities afforded by arcades seem obvious, with their crowds of teenagers who gather to watch each other play, trade game tips, or become the center of attention when it's their turn. Yet, according to many

40 experts, home video games provide their own unique opportunities for interaction among peers and family members. For example, they foster communication and cooperation between players, leading to a
45 joint effort to succeed. Some studies have shown that traditional age and gender gaps in game play of other types are modified or even eliminated during home video games.

For some youngsters, video game
50 prowess represents a way of gaining acceptance within their peer groups. David Brooks of the University of Southern California (USC) noted that those who, for various reasons, usually are left out of peer
55 group activities gain greater confidence as they master video games. This, in turn, encourages more socialization. Even those who never have been involved in video game research observe changes in their own
60 offspring. "An Allentown, Pa., couple . . . said their son's video games helped him through some difficult times. 'Our son is not an athletic type,' [the woman] said, 'but after he got the games, we noticed all the kids
65 started to congregate in our home. . . . It was his way of socializing.' "

In many homes, video games become a shared experience, opening new avenues of communication and discussion. They seem
70 to cut across age differences, even between parents and children. Psychologists Marianne and Stephen W. Garber and Robyn Freedman Spizman commented in an article in the *Atlanta Journal* that many parents
75 who never have experienced video games for themselves would find it rewarding to join their children in play. They will find that the youngsters "love the camaraderie and enjoy showing off [their] prowess." The

80 article also observes that, when they participate themselves, parents may be able to understand better why their children enjoy the games so much. As reporter Karen Paley observed in a recent article in

85 *The Boston Parents' Paper*, video games may be a channel for "our aggressive and competitive tendencies, and for relaxing, rather than wrestling, with our kids during this time in their lives."

—William B. White, Jr., excerpted from
"What Value Are Video Games?"
USA Today, March 1992

1. The writer wants to convince us that

    (1) children who play a lot of video games can get good jobs later in life
    (2) playing video games is the best form of home entertainment
    (3) children who spend time in video arcades are least likely to get into trouble
    (4) video games provide the best opportunities for interaction with peers and family
    (5) parents should learn the latest video games so they can enjoy a relaxing activity

2. The writer might agree that children who play video games a lot at home

    (1) become well-adjusted adults
    (2) get burned out at an early age
    (3) become addicted to Nintendo
    (4) need to get strong glasses
    (5) have difficulty relating to people

3. The excerpt is directed to which of the following groups of readers?

    (1) parents of adolescents
    (2) students in high school
    (3) children under twelve years of age
    (4) adults in computer classes
    (5) computer programmers

4. According to the writer, parents should join their children in playing video games to

    (1) monitor how they spend their time
    (2) get away from their own troubles
    (3) show them how to compete better
    (4) help increase their finger flexibility
    (5) improve communication through shared experiences

5. To find information for this article, the writer interviewed a

    (1) video arcade owner
    (2) computer designer
    (3) psychologist
    (4) teacher
    (5) game show host

ANSWERS ARE ON PAGE 302.

WRITING ACTIVITY 2

What games do you remember playing as a child? Choose one game that you played often. On a separate sheet of paper, describe the game. Explain why you enjoyed it. Then describe the skills or knowledge you gained from playing the game.

ANSWERS WILL VARY.

EXERCISE 7

Directions: Read the passage below and answer the questions that follow.

HOW DO SOAP OPERAS AFFECT TV VIEWERS?

Soap Operas: A Healthy Habit, After All?

Ever feel guilty about watching your favorite day-or-night soaps when "you really should be doing something worthwhile"? Consider this: psychologists say that watching soaps can benefit many people, provide a method of relaxation, a release from daily stresses, even a cure for
5 loneliness. Some psychotherapists even "prescribe" watching soaps to patients whose particular situation is being confronted by a show's characters. "It gives the person another way of thinking about the problem; and, in most cases, the more alternatives one has for solutions, the easier the problem will be to solve," said Mary Cassata, Ph.D., associate professor
10 of communications at the State University of New York at Buffalo.

"One of the reasons that soaps involve viewers so much is that the characters become a surrogate set of acquaintances," said Kenneth W. Haun, Ph.D., professor of psychology at Monmouth College in New Jersey, who teaches a course on soap operas. "A hundred years ago, you would
15 have tuned into your neighbors for gossip; but in today's more fragmented and alienated society, we can't do that as easily."

Unlike people, your soap opera "friends" can travel with you wherever there's a television set; and if you miss being with them one day or week, you can always catch up with them the next. This isn't to say that soap
20 opera characters should take the place of a person's real friends, but knowing they're there can be a comfort. Said Dr. Haun, "College students who are away from home for the first time report that one of the reasons they enjoy watching the soaps is that the characters are like friends from home. It makes them feel less lonely, less homesick."

25 Dr. Haun told of a New Jersey hospital in which nurses who check-in pregnant mothers ask the women if they have a favorite soap opera. If so, they try to match the woman with a roommate who watches the same show. "Usually the women stay in the hospital for days in a room with only one T.V.; and, normally, they don't talk very much. But if they watch the same
30 soap opera, they have a whole circle of friends in common."

Dr. Haun's research shows that soap opera audiences are generally about 65 percent female, 35 percent male, though the number of men

viewers is steadily climbing as is the number of viewers under thirty years
old. "Also, there doesn't seem to be any relationship between socio-
35 economic levels, occupations, or education among those who watch soaps,"
said Dr. Haun. "I know bank presidents who are hooked."

"People will watch soaps for years and remember the most minute
details," said Dr. Cassata. "That's because the viewers are made part of the
show; they're told secrets; they know what a character is thinking; they
40 know what a certain look means. And today, the characters have become
so complex, it's hard to tell the good guy from the bad guy; but that's often
the way life is."

—by Laura Flynn McCarthy

1. According to the first paragraph of the passage, what are three benefits of
watching soap operas?

(1) _____

(2) _____

(3) _____

2. Why do college students who are away from home watch soap operas?

_____

3. With which of the following statements would the author agree?

(1) People who watch soap operas should feel guilty.
(2) Watching soap operas causes quarreling among pregnant women.
(3) Soap opera characters are better friends than real people are.
(4) Soap operas are bad because they encourage gossip.
(5) Soap operas are therapeutic to those who watch them.

4. Based on the passage, choose *T* if the statement is true or *F* if the statement is
false.

T F **(1)** Most people who watch soap operas are uneducated housewives.

T F **(2)** Today's soap operas strictly divide characters into two distinct
types—"the good guys" and "the bad guys."

T F **(3)** According to Mary Cassata, Ph.D., a soap opera character's way of
solving a problem can be helpful to a member of the audience
who is experiencing a similar problem.

T F **(4)** The number of male soap opera watchers is decreasing.

5. Why does the author quote a psychology professor and a communications
professor? To

(1) demonstrate the author's high level of education
(2) support the author's opinion with experts' observations
(3) prove that the author communicates well
(4) show that only troubled people watch soap operas
(5) show that the author is a good listener

ANSWERS ARE ON PAGE 302.

SOCIAL ISSUES

The problem of missing children and the treatment of people with disabilities—two important social issues—are the subjects of the next two excerpts.

GED Practice
EXERCISE 8

Read the passage below and choose the best answer to each question that follows.

HAVE WE GONE TOO FAR?

Roger Pearson, a Detroit area teacher, was walking his dog when he saw a small boy fall off his bike. Pearson stopped to help him up, but the boy became terrified and
5 ran away and hid. "He was so scared of me," Pearson said, "he didn't even take his bike with him."

Nancy Zimmerman of Washington, D.C. drives three miles out of her way to shop at
10 a store that puts her groceries in plain bags. She also buys milk in plastic, gallon containers because the paper half gallons she used to buy all bear the pictures of missing children. "Every morning when they
15 eat breakfast, my kids don't need to see pictures of children who have been separated from their parents," she says. "Children feel powerless enough as it is."

America suddenly seems full of missing
15 children. Their faces are everywhere, on grocery store bags, on TV specials, on huge corporate-sponsored banners in children's clothing stores. Book and toy store shelves are flooded with books and games that warn
20 children against the "stranger danger." Companies selling personal alarms, insurance policies and dental identity disks have sprung up overnight. Safety programs have proliferated in schools promoting the
25 "yell and tell" message. Shopping centers host fingerprinting campaigns.

Surely one missing child is too many, but experts who work in the field of missing, sexually abused and runaway children say
30 the avalanche of publicity has grossly distorted the situation. Indeed, many feel that by overstating the problem we are poisoning relations between children and adults and creating a national paranoia that
35 may permanently damage the psyches of our children.

—Gini Hartzmark, excerpted from "Are We Filling Our Children with Fear?" *Chicago Tribune*, April 6, 1986

1. Who is Roger Pearson?

   (1) the parent of a missing child
   (2) a teacher who lives in the Detroit area
   (3) a detective who searches for missing children
   (4) an activist for children's rights
   (5) a person who has been convicted of kidnapping

2. The small boy ran away from Pearson because the boy

   (1) was riding a stolen bicycle
   (2) didn't want to go to the emergency room
   (3) was afraid Pearson wanted to harm him
   (4) feared Pearson would tell his parents he fell
   (5) had hit Pearson's dog with his bicycle

3. Why does Nancy Zimmerman buy milk in plastic containers instead of paper cartons?

(1) Plastic is a stronger material.
(2) Milk in plastic containers is cheaper.
(3) Milk spoils more quickly in paper cartons.
(4) Her grocery store doesn't sell milk in paper cartons.
(5) Pictures of missing children don't appear on plastic cartons.

4. What conclusion does the author reach about the topic?

(1) Because the issue of missing children is not a serious problem, publicity is unnecessary.
(2) Too much publicity about the problem of missing children is damaging to children and their relationships with adults.
(3) Many missing children are runaways, not kidnap victims.
(4) Fingerprinting children makes them feel like criminals.
(5) School safety programs effectively teach children how to avoid strangers.

ANSWERS ARE ON PAGE 302.

 **WRITING ACTIVITY 3**

In the preceding passage, you read about some tactics being used to address the problem of missing children. Do you believe that these tactics help to resolve the problem, or do they worsen the situation? Choose two of the following tactics. Then, on a separate sheet of paper, state and support your opinion on the effectiveness of each.

- Fingerprinting children
- School safety programs
- Children's pictures on milk cartons and grocery store bags
- Television specials
- Banners in children's stores
- Books and games about "stranger danger"

ANSWERS WILL VARY.

GED Practice
EXERCISE 9

Read the passage below and choose the best answer to each question that follows.

ARE PEOPLE INADVERTENTLY RUDE
TO THE DISABLED?

One of my friends runs etiquette
programs for business people. The last time
I went out with her, she was pushing my
wheelchair when she saw another friend.
5 She introduced us graciously—and then
they proceeded to carry on a conversation
above me.

There was no evil intent, but since I was
in my manual chair, I was not able to either
10 turn and join in the conversation or rejoin
the rest of our party. I sat and waited,
staring down the hall.

Ironically, I had helped write my friend's
business brochure two years ago, before
15 becoming disabled. Her programs address
different social situations, cultural clashes,
ages and sexes—but nothing in her sessions
relates to etiquette in dealing with the
disabled.

20 Unfortunately, many people—even the
most polite—need lessons on living, working
and generally interacting with the disabled.
In most cases, all that is required is some
thought or sensitivity.

25 When I was still getting out and about in
the business world, I used to enjoy meeting
up with a certain Philadelphia councilman at
various functions. Even though he is more
than a foot taller than I, he never loomed
30 over us shorter people. He always seemed
to find a way to bring the conversation to a
comfortable level, by leaning on a wall or
finding a seat.

When I later met his wife, in her
35 wheelchair, I discovered one secret to his
sensitivity.

For those of you who aren't accustomed
to being around someone with disabilities,
here are a few pointers.

40 • Don't park a wheelchair facing a wall.

• Be aware of where you leave a
wheelchair-bound person.

• Can they see and reach what they need,
such as a drink or reading material?
45 Those of us who can't stand get tired of
talking to belt buckles. Try to park us near
chairs or a low wall so people speaking
with us can be at our level. Cocktail
parties are the worst—extra effort must
50 be made to find a congenial spot for
conversation.

• Don't block curb cuts—ever.

That means even if you are a street
vendor just trying to make a buck or a
55 delivery man who will "just be a minute."

A high curb can be an insurmountable
obstacle for some people (I sat at one
intersection in downtown Philadelphia for
15 minutes one noon hour and counted five
60 people with wheelchairs, walkers or canes
that needed the low curb to cross the
street—one every three minutes). A simple
inconvenience for you might keep someone
else from a critical business or doctor's
65 appointment.

• Putting a ramp at the entrance isn't
enough if the bathroom door is too small.

The Americans with Disabilities Act
(ADA) is one year old now, so more
70 restaurants have ramps. A friend of mine
who is a quadriplegic and enjoys going out
for a few drinks with the boys has found lots
of bars that make it possible for him to come
in and spend his money.

75 However, getting to their bathrooms in a
wheelchair is impossible. Corners are too
sharp for turns, doorways and stalls are too
narrow. Those of us with primary caregivers
of the opposite sex need to be able to use a
80 simple, roomy, unisex facility.

- We are not all deaf, mute or mentally incapacitated—so don't treat us as if we were. Address us directly, in a normal voice, if you have a question—don't

85 assume someone else speaks for us. If necessary, most of us have developed some form of compensatory communication—lip reading, note writing, or in my case slow, deliberate speech.

90 I still think in complex compound sentences, but my disease affects my tongue movement, making it difficult to get words out quickly. Patience and attention are required.

95 The unifying theme of all the suggestions above is inclusiveness. We, the disabled, are part of the everyday world and wish to be treated accordingly—not as "special" or "different."

—Dale O'Reilley, excerpted from "Lessons in Living with the Disabled," *Chicago Tribune*, March 15, 1993

1. Which of the following statements summarizes the author's main message?

   (1) Getting into an ordinary bathroom in a wheelchair is impossible.
   (2) Always include a person who is in a wheelchair in your conversation.
   (3) More federal funding is needed for the disabled.
   (4) The Americans with Disabilities Act ensures equal access for people in wheelchairs.
   (5) People with disabilities want to be treated as part of the everyday world.

2. What does the writer mean when he says "I still think in complex compound sentences" (lines 90–91)?

   (1) He has normal, healthy intelligence.
   (2) He is smarter than most people.
   (3) People shout when speaking to a disabled person.
   (4) People should speak slowly to make sure the disabled person understands them.
   (5) His thought process is difficult to figure out.

3. In the first paragraph, the writer makes a point of telling us that his friend specializes in etiquette programs for businesspeople to show that

   (1) he has intelligent friends who know how to get along with people
   (2) he knows how to get out and make friends with interesting people
   (3) even experts in good manners may not know how to relate to the disabled
   (4) his friend always knows how to behave properly for all types of occasions
   (5) disabled people like her are able to run their own businesses

4. Which word best describes the writer's focus?

   (1) disability
   (2) friends
   (3) inclusiveness
   (4) obstacle
   (5) etiquette

5. Imagine that you are throwing a party. According to the excerpt, which of the following arrangements would be the most helpful to your wheelchair-bound guests?

   (1) politely requesting that your other guests give them preferential treatment
   (2) seating your other guests so that everyone is at the same eye level
   (3) making sure the disabled sit together at their own special table
   (4) directing questions and comments to disabled persons' caregivers
   (5) speaking more loudly, slowly, and distinctly than you normally do

ANSWERS ARE ON PAGE 302.

MORE ON NONFICTION PROSE

The following excerpts give you more practice in understanding nonfiction prose. The first selection deals with the capture of legendary criminal John Dillinger. The second is a description of an Oklahoma scene.

EXERCISE 10

Directions: Read the passage below and answer the questions that follow.

HOW WAS A FAMOUS CRIMINAL SHOT?

John Dillinger, ace bad man of the world, got his last night—two slugs through his heart and one through his head. He was tough and he was shrewd, but wasn't as tough and shrewd as the Federals, who never close a case until the end. It took twenty-seven of them to end Dillinger's career,
5 and their strength came out of his weakness—a woman.

Dillinger was put on the spot by a tip-off to the local bureau of the Department of Justice. It was a feminine voice that Melvin H. Purvis, head of the Chicago office, heard. He had waited long for it.

It was Sunday, but Uncle Sam doesn't observe any NRA* and works
10 seven days a week.

The voice told him that Dillinger would be at a little third-run movie house, the Biograph, last night— that he went there every night and usually got there about 7:30. It was almost 7:30 then. Purvis sent out a call for all men within reach and hustled all men on hand with him. They waited more
15 than an hour. They knew from the informer that he must come out, turn left, turn again into a dark alley where he parked his Ford-8 coupe.

Purvis himself stood at the main exit. He had men on foot and in parked inconspicuous cars strung on both sides of the alley. He was to give the signal. He had ascertained about when the feature film, *Manhattan*
20 *Melodrama*, would end. Tensely eying his wrist watch he stood. Then the crowd that always streams out when the main picture finishes came. Purvis had seen Dillinger when he was brought through from Arizona to Crown Point, Indiana, and his heart pounded as he saw again the face that has been studied by countless millions on the front pages of the world.

25 Purvis gave the signal. Dillinger did not see him. Public Enemy No. 1 lit a cigarette, strolled a few feet to the alley with the mass of middle-class citizens going in that direction, then wheeled left.

A Federal man, revolver in hand, stepped from behind a telegraph pole at the mouth of the passage. "Hello, John," he said, almost whispered, his
30 voice husky with the intensity of the classic melodrama. Dillinger went with lightning right hand for his gun, a .38 Colt automatic. He drew it from his trousers pocket.

*National Recovery Administration (NRA), a New Deal agency that, among other functions, regulated the hours of work in industry.

But, from behind, another government agent pressed the muzzle of his service revolver against Dillinger's back and fired twice. Both bullets went
35 through the bandit's heart.

He staggered, his weapon clattered to the asphalt paving, and as he went three more shots flashed. One bullet hit the back of his head, downward, as he was falling, and came out under his eye.

Police cleared the way for the police car which was there in a few
40 minutes. The police were there not because they were in on the capture, but because the sight of so many mysterious men around the theater had scared the manager into thinking he was about to be stuck up and he had called the nearest station.

—Excerpted from "Dillinger 'Gets His' " by Jack Lait

1. The shooting occurred in

(1) Arizona
(2) Chicago
(3) Indiana
(4) New York
(5) Washington, D.C.

2. *Manhattan Melodrama* is the title of a

(1) play
(2) short story
(3) soap opera
(4) classical symphony
(5) movie

3. The author's style of language can be compared with a

(1) police report
(2) criminal law textbook
(3) gangster novel
(4) medical diagnosis
(5) horror movie script

4. The following events are arranged in jumbled order. Rearrange the events in the order in which they happen in the passage. Number the sentences 1–6 to show the correct sequence.

_____ Purvis gave the signal to his men.

_____ Dillinger drew his gun on a Federal man.

_____ Purvis and his men were stationed around the Biograph theater.

_____ A police car arrived shortly after the shooting.

_____ Another government agent shot Dillinger in the back.

_____ A woman informer tipped off Purvis.

ANSWERS ARE ON PAGE 302.

EXERCISE 11

Directions: Read the passage below and answer the questions that follow.

WHAT DOES A PLAIN LOOK LIKE?

A single knoll rises out of the plain in Oklahoma, north and west of the Wichita range. For my people, the Kiowas, it is an old landmark, and they gave it the name Rainy Mountain. The hardest weather in the world is there. Winter brings blizzards, hot tornadic winds arise in the spring, and in the
5 summer the prairie is an anvil's edge. The grass turns brittle and brown, and it cracks beneath your feet. There are green belts along the rivers and creeks, linear groves of hickory and pecan, willow and witch hazel. At a distance in July or August the steaming foliage seems almost to writhe in fire. Great green and yellow grasshoppers are everywhere in the tall grass,
10 popping up like corn to sting the flesh, and tortoises crawl about on the red earth, going nowhere in the plenty of time. Loneliness is an aspect of the land. All things in the plain are isolate; there is no confusion of objects in the eye, but *one* hill or *one* tree or *one* man. To look upon that landscape in the early morning, with the sun at your back, is to lose the sense of
15 proportion. Your imagination comes to life, and this, you think, is where Creation was begun.

—Excerpted from "The Way to Rainy Mountain" by N. Scott Momaday

1. What is the name of the author's Indian tribe? _____

2. Write a phrase from the passage that appeals to each of the senses:

Sight: _____   Hearing: _____   Touch: _____

3. The author states "the steaming foliage seems almost to writhe in fire" (lines 8–9) to

(1) emphasize the intense summer heat
(2) suggest that forest fires are commonplace
(3) describe the fiery sunset
(4) explain the effects of daylight on plant growth
(5) show that Native Americans worship the sun

4. The author's description of the plain can be compared with a

(1) weather report
(2) map of Oklahoma
(3) passage from the Bible
(4) landscape painting
(5) real estate brochure

5. You can infer that the word *knoll* (line 1) means a

(1) hill
(2) landmark
(3) blizzard
(4) tornado
(5) prairie

ANSWERS ARE ON PAGE 302.

NONFICTION PROSE

Read each passage below and answer the questions that follow.

Questions 1–6 refer to the following excerpt from an article.

HOW DOES A POLICE ARTIST PERFORM HIS JOB?

Initially, Mr. Hagenlocher tries to put witnesses at ease so they trust him, rather than barging up and identifying himself as a police officer. When questioning someone,
5 the artist tries to exact as much detail as possible about the suspect, though he can get by on remarkably few facts. As a rule, he looks for five features: shape of face, hair, eyes, ears, and mouth. Distinguishing scars,
10 birthmarks, beards, and mustaches are an artist's dream for producing a useful sketch, but they don't often crop up.

Mr. Hagenlocher always carts along 150 to 200 of the 900,000 mug shots the police
15 force keeps. Witnesses are asked to leaf through these to try to find a similar face, and then subtle changes can be made in the sketch. "You could use just one photo and work from that," Mr. Hagenlocher says.
20 "Using that as a base, you have the witness compare the hair—is it longer or shorter?— the mouth—is it thinner or wider?—and so forth. But that's harder and takes more time. It's usually much quicker to show him a lot
25 of photos and have them pick the one that's close."

"But I remember one time," the artist goes on, "when a girl flipped through a mess of photos and finally picked one. 'That looks
30 exactly like him,' she said, 'except the hair was longer, the mouth was wider, the eyes were further apart, the nose was smaller, and the face was rounder.' She was a big help."

35 Besides the five basic features, Mr. Hagenlocher also questions witnesses about a suspect's apparent nationality and the nature of the language he used. This can be of subtle assistance in sketching the
40 suspect, but it can also sometimes link several sketches together. For instance, if over a short period of time three suspects are described as soft-spoken, in addition to having other similar traits, then chances are
45 they are the same person. It is also a good idea to ask a witness if a suspect resembled a famous person. Suspects have been compared to Marlon Brando, Rod Steiger, Winston Churchill, Nelson Eddy, Jack
50 Palance, Jackie Gleason, Mick Jagger and a Greek god.

After Mr. Hagenlocher completes a sketch, he shows it to the witness or witnesses for their reaction. Usually, there
55 will be lots of minor, and sometimes not too minor, changes to be made. When it's finished, the sketch isn't intended to approach the polished form of a portrait. "We're just trying to narrow down the
60 possibilities," Mr. Hagenlocher says. "If you've just got a big nose and a thin mouth to go with, then at least you've ruled out all the people with small noses and thick mouths. There are still millions of people still
65 in the running, but millions have also been eliminated."

—N. R. Kleinfield, excerpted from "Portraits of a Cop," *Wall Street Journal*, April 1970

1. The major purpose of the entire passage is to

   (1) analyze witnesses' observations
   (2) explain the process of sketching a suspect
   (3) classify different types of suspects
   (4) compare drawing to photography
   (5) describe how witnesses remember faces

2. When Mr. Hagenlocher first meets witnesses, what does he do? He

   (1) badgers them with questions
   (2) emphasizes that he is a police officer
   (3) mistrusts their descriptions
   (4) makes them feel comfortable
   (5) evaluates their intelligence

CONTINUED

3. Why do witnesses examine mug shots? To

   (1) determine whether the suspect is a former convicted criminal
   (2) find faces similar to the suspect's
   (3) test their photographic memories
   (4) study criminal-looking faces
   (5) observe how criminals pose for photographs

4. Which of the following questions would Mr. Hagenlocher *not* ask a witness?

   (1) Does the suspect resemble a famous person?
   (2) What is the suspect's apparent nationality?
   (3) How does the suspect use language?
   (4) Was the suspect armed?
   (5) Does the suspect have a distinguishing birthmark?

5. Which of the following techniques does the author use to develop the topic?

   (1) the court testimony of witnesses
   (2) interviews with arrested suspects
   (3) a description of a notorious suspect
   (4) excerpts from an official police report
   (5) quotations from Mr. Hagenlocher

6. Of the following people, the person who could most closely identify with Mr. Hagenlocher's work is a

   (1) photographer
   (2) plastic surgeon
   (3) portrait painter
   (4) film director
   (5) sculptor

Questions 7–11 refer to the following excerpt from a speech.

WHAT DID A PRESIDENT EXPECT FROM US?

In your hands, my fellow citizens, more than mine, will rest the final success or failure of our course. Since this country was founded, each generation of Americans has
5 been summoned to give testimony to its national loyalty. . . .

Now the trumpet summons us again— not as a call to bear arms, though arms we need—not as a call to battle, though
10 embattled we are—but a call to bear the burden of a long twilight struggle, year in and year out, "rejoicing in hope, patient in tribulation"—a struggle against the common enemies of man: Tyranny, poverty, disease
15 and war itself.

Can we forge against these enemies a grand and global alliance, North and South, East and West, that can assure a more fruitful life for all mankind? Will you join in
20 that historic effort?

In the long history of the world, only a few generations have been granted the role of defending freedom in its hour of maximum danger.

25 I do not shrink from this responsibility—I welcome it. I do not believe that any of us would exchange places with any other people or any other generation. The energy, the faith, the devotion which we bring to this
30 endeavor will light our country and all who serve it—and the glow from that fire can truly light the world.

And so, my fellow Americans: Ask not
what your country can do for you—ask what
35 you can do for your country.

My fellow citizens of the world: Ask not
what America will do for you, but what
together we can do for the freedom of man.

Finally, whether you are citizens of
40 America or citizens of the world, ask of us
here the same high standards of strength
and sacrifice which we ask of you. With a
good conscience our only sure reward, with
history the final judge of our deeds, let us
45 go forth to lead the land we love, asking His
blessing and His help, but knowing that here
on earth God's work must truly be our own.

—John F. Kennedy, excerpted from
"Inaugural Address," 1960

7. What is the main idea of the passage?

(1) War and poverty are our worst enemies.
(2) The American people are responsible for
the fate of the nation.
(3) Americans are selfishly preoccupied with
their individual problems.
(4) Military strength is necessary in the
struggle for freedom.
(5) Only the president of the United States
can solve the country's problems.

8. John F. Kennedy states that during the course
of American history, each generation has
demonstrated its

(1) freedom of speech
(2) fear of illness
(3) financial success
(4) national loyalty
(5) hatred toward foreign countries

9. The tone of the speech is intended to be

(1) frightening
(2) overemotional
(3) inspiring
(4) tragic
(5) argumentative

10. According to this passage, what is John F.
Kennedy's attitude toward the presidency?

(1) He is overwhelmed by the enormous
responsibilities.
(2) He enthusiastically accepts the
challenges of leadership.
(3) He is greedy with power and wants total
control of the government.
(4) He welcomes the opportunity to build the
military.
(5) He looks forward to shaping economic
policies.

11. The writing style of the concluding sentence
resembles the language used in a

(1) newscaster's report
(2) lawyer's appeal
(3) preacher's sermon
(4) historian's analysis
(5) magazine advertisement

Questions 12–18 refer to the following excerpt from an autobiography.

HOW DID MALCOLM X IMPROVE HIMSELF DURING HIS PRISON TERM?

The Norfolk Prison Colony's library was in the school building. A variety of classes was taught there by instructors who came from such places as Harvard and Boston
5 universities. The weekly debates between inmate teams were also held in the school building. You would be astonished to know how worked up convict debaters and audiences would get over subjects like
10 "Should Babies Be Fed Milk?"

Available on the prison library's shelves were books on just about every general subject. Much of the big private collection that Parkhurst had willed to the prison was
15 still in crates and boxes in the back of the library—thousands of old books. Some of them looked ancient: covers faded, old-time parchment-looking binding. Parkhurst, I've mentioned, seemed to have been principally
20 interested in history and religion. He had the money and the special interest to have a lot of books that you wouldn't have in general circulation. Any college library would have been lucky to get that collection.

25 As you can imagine, especially in a prison where there was heavy emphasis on rehabilitation, an inmate was smiled upon if he demonstrated an unusually intense interest in books. There was a sizable
30 number of well-read inmates, especially the popular debaters. Some were said by many to be practically walking encyclopedias. They were almost celebrities. No university would ask any student to devour literature as
35 I did when this new world opened to me, of being able to read and *understand*.

I read more in my room than in the library itself. An inmate who was known to read a lot could check out more than the
40 permitted maximum number of books. I preferred reading in the total isolation of my own room.

When I had progressed to really serious reading, every night at about ten P.M. I
45 would be outraged with the "lights out." It always seemed to catch me right in the middle of something engrossing.

Fortunately, right outside my door was a corridor light that cast a glow into my room.
50 The glow was enough to read by, once my eyes adjusted to it. So when "lights out" came, I would sit on the floor where I could continue reading in that glow.

—Malcolm X with Alex Haley, excerpted from
The Autobiography of Malcolm X, 1964

12. Who taught the academic classes at the prison?

(1) prison guards
(2) librarians
(3) college-educated convicts
(4) professional debaters
(5) university instructors

13. Based on information in the excerpt, you can infer that the weekly debates between teams of inmates were

(1) popular with the inmate debaters and their audiences
(2) dangerous to guards because the debates often became heated
(3) fun for Mr. Parkhurst and other influential people who came to watch
(4) frustrating to inmate debaters, who did not have access to books
(5) discouraged by the prison system, which viewed them as a waste of time

14. What was the prison officials' reaction to inmates who were interested in books?

(1) suspicious
(2) critical
(3) indifferent
(4) approving
(5) surprised

15. Why does Malcolm X refer to certain inmates as "walking encyclopedias" (line 32)? They

   (1) were responsible for carrying books
   (2) used to sell encyclopedias door to door
   (3) were well informed on a variety of topics
   (4) paced around the library while they read
   (5) liked to exercise their minds

16. Why was Malcolm X annoyed with the "lights out" rule at 10:00 P.M.?

   (1) He was afraid of the dark.
   (2) He had difficulties falling asleep.
   (3) His reading was interrupted.
   (4) He was outraged with unfair prison regulations.
   (5) He disliked childish treatment.

17. What is the major point that Malcolm X expresses in the passage? His

   (1) respect for his fellow inmates
   (2) enthusiasm for reading and learning
   (3) support of rehabilitating convicts
   (4) attitude toward the prison system
   (5) interest in books about history and religion

18. If Malcolm X were alive today, which of the following statements would he most likely support?

   (1) Classroom instruction is not effective.
   (2) Debates often result in arguments.
   (3) People have the ability to educate themselves.
   (4) Prison libraries are poorly stocked.
   (5) University students know less than self-taught convicts.

ANSWERS ARE ON PAGE 303.

*Critics have hailed Toni Morrison as one of the best fiction writers of our time.
She won the Nobel Prize for literature in 1993.*

5 Prose Fiction

Fiction writers invent a self-contained world where imaginary events unfold. Writers also create characters who play a role in these events. On the GED Literature and the Arts Test, you will read excerpts from two types of fiction—the novel and the short story. The novel is a book-length story, a fully developed portrayal of people, situations, and places. Because it is more concise, the short story usually focuses on one major event or a series of closely related incidents. In this chapter, you will study the following elements of fictional prose:

- setting
- plot
- point of view
- characterization
- figurative language
- theme

Understanding these elements will help you analyze and interpret fiction.

SETTING

Fiction writers stage the action of their stories by establishing *setting*— the place, the time, and the atmosphere in which dramatic situations occur.

The *place* roots the action to a specific location or geographical area. For example, the following list identifies some of the places described in short stories and novels:

- a bingo parlor
- a supermarket
- a roadside diner
- a jungle island off the Brazilian coast
- a small town in Ohio
- a southern plantation

The *time* frames the action of the story by explaining when the events happened—the time of day, the season, or the historical period. Ralph Ellison's short story "King of the Bingo Game" takes place in the evening. John Updike's short story "A & P" occurs during the summer. F. Scott Fitzgerald's novel *The Great Gatsby* is set in the 1920s.

The **atmosphere** conveys the emotions associated with the story's physical environment. Descriptions of specific places often create the atmosphere. An intimate, candle-lit restaurant may evoke romantic feelings. The emotions associated with funeral parlors are grief and loss.

Apply your understanding of the terms *place*, *time*, and *atmosphere* as you read the following paragraph:

> It was raining that morning, and still very dark. When the boy reached the streetcar café he had almost finished his route and he went in for a cup of coffee. The place was an all-night café owned by a bitter and stingy man called Leo. After the raw, empty street the café seemed friendly and bright: along the counter there were a couple of soldiers, three spinners from the cotton mill, and in a corner a man who sat hunched over with his nose and half his face down in a beer mug.

> —Excerpted from "A Tree. A Rock. A Cloud"
> by Carson McCullers

In the following spaces, identify the three elements of setting:

Place: _____

Time of day: _____

Atmosphere of the place: _____

If you wrote that the scene occurs in the morning at a streetcar café, you correctly named the time and the place. The phrase *friendly and bright* describes the atmosphere of the café.

In the preceding excerpt, you see a young boy and some customers. The fictional setting provides the background in which characters enact the events of the story.

HOW AUTHORS ESTABLISH SETTING

As you noticed in the excerpt from "A Tree. A Rock. A Cloud," the author tells you the place, the time, and the atmosphere. Sometimes, authors directly state these elements of setting. Here are some examples.

DIRECT STATEMENTS OF PLACE

We went to the only nightclub on a short, dark street, downtown.

> —Excerpted from "Sonny's Blues" by James Baldwin

The village of Loma is built, as its name implies, on a low round hill that rises like an island out of the flat mouth of the Salinas Valley in central California.

> —Excerpted from "Johnny Bear" by John Steinbeck

Murphy slams the phone down and bounds back upstairs to his room in the YMCA to sit alone. . . .

—Excerpted from "Murphy's Xmas" by Mark Costello

The military School of St. Severin. The gymnasium. The class in their white cotton shirts stand in two rows under the big gas lights.

—Excerpted from "Gym Period" by Rainer Maria Rilke

DIRECT STATEMENTS OF TIME

I sit in the sun drinking gin. It is ten in the morning.

—Excerpted from "The Fourth Alarm" by John Cheever

It was the second day of Easter week.

—Excerpted from "The Peasant Marey"
by Fyodor Dostoyevsky

The morning of June 27th was clear and sunny, with the fresh warmth of a full-summer day. . . .

—Excerpted from "The Lottery" by Shirley Jackson

It was December—a bright frozen day in the early morning.

—Excerpted from "A Worn Path" by Eudora Welty

DIRECT STATEMENTS OF ATMOSPHERE

The oiler swung the boat then and, seated in the stern, the cook and the correspondent were obliged to look over their shoulders to contemplate the lonely and indifferent shore.

—Excerpted from "The Open Boat" by Stephen Crane

The room in which I found myself was very large and lofty. . . . I felt that I breathed an atmosphere of sorrow. An air of stern, deep, and irredeemable gloom hung over and pervaded all.

—Excerpted from "The Fall of the House of Usher"
by Edgar Allan Poe

INFERRING PLACE AND TIME

When authors do not name the place or time, you can infer this information from descriptive details. Infer where the action in the following paragraph occurs.

> The pass was high and wide and he jumped for it, feeling it slap flatly against his hands, as he shook his hips to throw off the halfback who was driving at him. The center floated by, his hands desperately brushing Darling's knee as Darling picked his feet up high and delicately ran over a blocker and an opposing linesman in a jumble on the ground near the scrimmage line.
>
> —Excerpted from "The Eighty Yard Run"
> by Irwin Shaw

If you said "a football field," you were correct. What are some of the clues that support this inference? Write the words or phrases on the following lines:

_____   _____

_____   _____

Pass, halfback, blocker, and *scrimmage line* all refer to football. You can conclude that the men are playing this sport on a football field.

In the next example, the author does not tell the reader the era in which the story is set. However, you can infer the historical period from the description of the main character, a man who is hanged for treason.

> Peyton Farquhar was a well-to-do planter, of an old and highly respectable Alabama family. Being a slave owner and like other slave owners a politician he was naturally an original secessionist and ardently devoted to the Southern cause.
>
> —Excerpted from "An Occurrence at Owl Creek Bridge"
> by Ambrose Bierce

What clues from the character description suggest that the story happens during the Civil War years? On the following lines, write two phrases that support this inference about setting:

_____

_____

As you probably noted, Peyton Farquhar is a "slave owner" who is "devoted to the Southern cause," which included preserving the institution of slavery.

INFERRING ATMOSPHERE

Recall that *atmosphere* refers to the emotional qualities associated with a place. An author usually suggests an atmosphere by describing the physical appearance of a place or by showing how characters react to their environment.

The following paragraph describes an abandoned house. Notice the feelings conveyed by the descriptive language.

> On a night the wind loosened a shingle and flipped it to the ground. The next wind pried into the hole where the shingle had been, lifted off three, and the next, a dozen. The midday sun burned through the hole and threw a glaring spot on the floor. The wild cats crept in from the fields at night, but they did not mew at the doorstep any more. They moved like shadows of a cloud across the moon, into the rooms to hunt the mice. And on windy nights the doors banged, and the ragged curtains fluttered in the broken windows.
>
> —Excerpted from *The Grapes of Wrath* by John Steinbeck

This excerpt illustrates how the sun and the wind are gradually destroying the empty house. What is your impression of the atmosphere? Desolate? Bleak? Dreary? These are some of the words that capture the overall feeling of this place. John Steinbeck, the author, conveys the atmosphere through images relating to sights and sounds. Reread his concluding sentence. Try to imagine hearing doors banging on a windy night and seeing ragged curtains fluttering in broken windows.

WRITING ACTIVITY 1

Where would you like to be at this moment? At the beach? In the mountains? At a party with friends and family? On a separate sheet of paper, write a paragraph describing the setting and atmosphere of the scene you envision. Use plenty of descriptive details to make your paragraph vivid.

ANSWERS WILL VARY.

≡ **GED Practice** ≡
EXERCISE 1

Read the passage below and choose the best answer to each question that follows.

WHAT DO THE CHILDREN HEAR?

And so the house came to be haunted
by the unspoken phrase: There must be
more money! There must be more money!
The children could hear it all the time,
5 though nobody said it aloud. They heard it
at Christmas, when the expensive and
splendid toys filled the nursery. Behind the
shining modern rocking-horse, behind the
smart doll's house, a voice would start
10 whispering: "There must be more money!
There must be more money!" And the
children would stop playing, to listen for a
moment. They would look into each other's
eyes, to see if they had all heard. And each
15 one saw in the eyes of the other two that
they too had heard. "There must be more
money! There must be more money!"

It came whispering from the springs of
the still-swaying rocking-horse, and even the
20 horse, bending his wooden, champing head,
heard it. The big doll, sitting so pink and
smirking in her new pram, could hear it quite
plainly, and seemed to be smirking all the
more self-consciously because of it. The
25 foolish puppy, too, that took the place of the
teddy-bear, he was looking so
extraordinarily foolish for no other reason
but that he heard the secret whisper all over
the house: "There must be more money!"

30 Yet nobody ever said it aloud. The
whisper was everywhere, and therefore no
one spoke it. Just as no one ever says: "We
are breathing!" in spite of the fact that
breath is coming and going all the time.

—D. H. Lawrence, excerpted from "The
Rocking-Horse Winner," 1926

1. Which of the following statements about the
   children is true?

   (1) They wish they had more toys.
   (2) They fear running short of money.
   (3) Their house is haunted by ghosts.
   (4) They don't take care of their possessions.
   (5) Their whispering annoys their parents.

2. Where does the action described in the
   excerpt take place?

   (1) in a school
   (2) on a playground
   (3) at a toy store
   (4) in a daycare center
   (5) in a nursery

3. Which word best describes the atmosphere of
   the house?

   (1) peaceful
   (2) cheerful
   (3) tense
   (4) joyous
   (5) angry

ANSWERS ARE ON PAGE 303.

EXERCISE 2

Directions: Read the passage below and answer the questions that follow.

It was freezing cold, with a fog that caught your breath. Two large searchlights were crisscrossing over the compound from the watchtowers at the far corners. The lights on the perimeter and the lights inside the camp were on full force. There were so many of them that they blotted out the stars.

With their felt boots crunching on the snow, prisoners were rushing past on their business—to the latrines, to the supply rooms, to the package room, or to the kitchen to get their groats cooked. Their shoulders were hunched and their coats buttoned up, and they all felt cold, not so much because of the freezing weather as because they knew they'd have to be out in it all day. But the Tartar in his old overcoat with shabby blue tabs walked steadily on and the cold didn't seem to bother him at all.

They went past the high wooden fence around the punishment block (the stone prison inside the camp), past the barbed-wire fence that guarded the bakery from the prisoners, past the corner of the HQ where a length of frost-covered rail was fastened to a post with heavy wire, and past another post where—in a sheltered spot to keep the readings from being too low—the thermometer hung, caked over with ice. Shukhov gave a hopeful sidelong glance at the milk-white tube. If it went down to forty-two below zero they weren't supposed to be marched out to work. But today the thermometer wasn't pushing forty or anything like it.

—Excerpted from *One Day in the Life of Ivan Denisovich*
by Alexander Solzhenitsyn

1. The story most likely takes place in

   (1) a military academy
   (2) an army post
   (3) a prison camp
   (4) a combat zone
   (5) a reform school

2. The atmosphere depicted in this passage is

   (1) violent
   (2) suspenseful
   (3) dull
   (4) hopeful
   (5) oppressive

3. List four phrases referring to the weather. _____

_____

_____

ANSWERS ARE ON PAGE 303.

PLOT

The *plot* of a story refers to the action—the sequence of events. A writer structures and organizes events to suit the purpose of the story he or she wants to tell. As author John Steinbeck once explained, "Of course, a writer rearranges life, shortens the intervals, sharpens events, and devises beginnings, middles, and ends." In other words, writers present an organized version of experiences that may occur in real life.

In fiction, the action progresses toward a believable conclusion. Individual incidents or episodes are connected logically. For example, the events may unfold in a series of cause-and-effect relationships. When you are reading a fictional passage, ask yourself why an event happened, what the outcome was, and what will happen next.

Summarizing the action of a scene can also help you see how plot details are related. Identify the main incident described in the excerpt.

The dogs were cast, still on leash. They struck immediately. The trail was good, easily followed because of the dew. The fugitive had apparently made no effort whatever to hide it. They could even see the prints of his knees and hands where he had knelt to drink from a spring. "I never yet knew a murderer that had more sense than that about the folks that would chase him," the deputy said. "But this durn fool dont even suspect that we might use dogs."

"We been putting dogs on him once a day ever since Sunday," the sheriff said. "And we aint caught him yet."

"Them were cold trails. We aint had a good hot trail until today. But he's made his mistake at last. We'll get him today. Before noon, maybe."

"I'll wait and see, I reckon," the sheriff said.

"You'll see," the deputy said. "This trail is running straight as a railroad. I could follow it, myself almost. Look here. You can even see his footprints. The durn fool aint even got enough sense to get into the road, in the dust, where other folks have walked and where the dogs cant scent him. Them dogs will find the end of them footprints before ten o'clock."

Which the dogs did. Presently the trail bent sharply at right angles. They followed it and came onto a road, which they followed behind the lowheaded and eager dogs who, after a short distance, swung to the roadside where a path came down from a cotton house in a nearby field. They began to bay, milling, tugging, their voices loud, mellow, ringing; whining and surging with excitement. "Why, the durn fool!" the deputy said. "He set down here and rested: here's his footmarks: them same rubber heels. He aint a mile ahead right now! Come on, boys!" They went on, the leashes taut, the dogs baying, the men moving now at a trot.

—Excerpted from *Light in August* by William Faulkner

Which statement best summarizes the action of this passage?

(1) A murderer runs away from the law.
(2) A fugitive outsmarts the sheriff and his deputy.
(3) A sheriff, a deputy, and his dogs try to track down a murderer.
(4) A sheriff and his deputy disagree on plans for a manhunt.
(5) The dogs are useless in capturing the fugitive.

Answer (3) is the right response. The entire scene traces the sheriff, the deputy, and the dogs' pursuit of the murderer. Answer (1) describes the reason for the manhunt, but does not summarize the action. Answers (2) and (5) are possible outcomes, but they are not the main action in the passage. Answer (4) describes a specific moment from the scene.

As you read the passage, did you also notice that the setting changes? The author reveals this shift in location by showing where the sheriff and his deputy have found the fugitive's handprints and footmarks. Study the passage again. On the following lines, describe the locations where the passage begins and ends:

1. _____   2. _____

The two locations are 1. an area near a spring and 2. a path coming down from a cotton house in a nearby field.

CONFLICT IN PLOT

Headlines often report *conflicts*—clashes between opposing forces:

Hurricane Off Florida Coastline Forces Residents to Evacuate

Professional Athlete Struggles to Overcome Drug Problems

Citizens Stage Protest Against Nuclear Weapons and the Arms Race

Two Men Arrested in Barroom Brawl

**Negotiations Continue Between Striking Teachers and
Board of Education**

Movie Star Tells About Battle to Recover from Stroke

As these newspaper headlines illustrate, conflict is a part of everyday life. People find themselves at odds with their environment, society, or other individuals. They also confront personal problems that result in inner conflicts. These kinds of real-life conflicts also occur in fictional plots.

The events of a story often arise when characters defy society or other individuals, cope with dangerous surroundings, or struggle with their own emotions. These conflicts create moments of tension in the plot.

The following excerpt from Richard Wright's novel *Native Son* shows Bigger, the main character, in a conflict.

A huge black rat squealed and leaped at Bigger's trouser-leg and snagged it in his teeth, hanging on.

"Goddamn!" Bigger whispered fiercely, whirling and kicking out his leg with all the strength of his body. The force of his movement shook the rat loose and it sailed through the air and struck a wall. Instantly, it rolled over and leaped again. Bigger dodged and the rat landed against a table leg. With clenched teeth, Bigger held the skillet; he was afraid to hurl it, fearing that he might miss. The rat squeaked and turned and ran in a narrow circle, looking for a place to hide; it leaped again past Bigger and scurried on dry rasping feet to one side of the box and then to the other, searching for the hole. Then it turned and reared upon its hind legs.

"Hit 'im, Bigger!" Buddy shouted.

"Kill 'im!" the woman screamed.

The rat's belly pulsed with fear. Bigger advanced a step and the rat emitted a long thin song of defiance, its black beady eyes glittering, its tiny forefeet pawing the air restlessly. Bigger swung the skillet; it skidded over the floor, missing the rat, and clattered to a stop against a wall.

"Goddamn!"

The rat leaped. Bigger sprang to one side. The rat stopped under a chair and let out a furious screak. Bigger moved slowly backward toward the door.

"Gimme that skillet, Buddy," he asked quietly, not taking his eyes from the rat.

Buddy extended his hand. Bigger caught the skillet and lifted it high in the air. The rat scuttled across the floor and stopped again at the box and searched quickly for the hole; then it reared once more and bared long yellow fangs, piping shrilly, belly quivering.

Bigger aimed and let the skillet fly with a heavy grunt. There was a shattering of wood as the box caved in. The woman screamed and hid her face in her hands. Bigger tiptoed forward and peered.

"I got 'im," he muttered, his clenched teeth bared in a smile. "By God, I got 'im."

On the lines, state the conflict and explain how it was resolved.

The conflict is between _____ and the _____.

The conflict was resolved when _____.

Bigger resolved the conflict between himself and the rat by killing it.

GED Practice
EXERCISE 3

The following excerpt is from a short story set in South Africa, where apartheid, the official policy of racial segregation, was strictly enforced. The laws under apartheid denied blacks certain human rights. As you read the excerpt, be aware of how the setting influences Karlie and his actions. Then choose the best answer to each question that follows.

WHAT DOES THE BENCH MEAN?

Here was his challenge! *The bench.* The railway bench with "Europeans Only" neatly painted on it in white. For one moment it symbolized all the misery of the plural South
5 African society.

Here was his challenge to the rights of a man. Here it stood. A perfectly ordinary wooden railway bench, like thousands of others in South Africa. His challenge. That
10 bench now had concentrated in it all the evils of a system he could not understand and he felt a victim of. It was the obstacle between himself and humanity. If he sat on it, he was a man. If he was afraid he denied
15 himself membership as a human being in a human society. He almost had visions of righting this pernicious system, if he only sat down on that bench. Here was his chance. He, Karlie, would challenge.

20 He seemed perfectly calm when he sat down on the bench, but inside his heart was thumping wildly. Two conflicting ideas now throbbed through him. The one said, "I have no right to sit on this bench." The other was
25 the voice of a new religion and said, "Why have I no right to sit on this bench?" The one voice spoke of the past, of the servile position he had occupied on the farm, of his father, and his father's father who were born
30 black, lived like blacks, and died like mules. The other voice spoke of new horizons and said, "Karlie, you are a man. You have dared what your father and your father's father would not have dared. You will die like a
35 man."

—Richard Rive, excerpted from "The Bench," 1960

1. In Karlie's eyes, what does the bench represent?

   (1) a peaceful place to rest
   (2) the European railway system
   (3) an unreasonable fear of whites
   (4) the importance of obeying the law
   (5) the pain of racial segregation

2. Karlie's inner conflict in paragraph 3 is triggered by an outside conflict with

   (1) his father
   (2) his grandfather
   (3) South African society
   (4) the bench
   (5) European police

3. Which of the following words best describes Karlie's behavior?

   (1) calm
   (2) courageous
   (3) reckless
   (4) silly
   (5) cowardly

4. If Karlie were living in the United States today, he would probably support

   (1) people opposed to school busing
   (2) stronger law enforcement
   (3) financial aid to foreign countries
   (4) discrimination against protesters
   (5) the human rights movement

ANSWERS ARE ON PAGE 304.

WRITING ACTIVITY 2

On a separate sheet of paper, write about a conflict from your own experience. Some suggested topics include (1) a conflict with another person—a relative, a friend, a boss, or an enemy; (2) an inner conflict about making a decision—getting married, returning to school, or breaking a rule. Organize your paragraphs by answering each of these questions:

Paragraph 1: What were the two opposing sides of the conflict?

Paragraph 2: What caused the conflict?

Paragraph 3: What tense moments did the conflict create?

ANSWERS WILL VARY.

POINT OF VIEW

When you read stories, through whose eyes do you see the setting, the plot, and the characters? Sometimes, an author chooses to tell a story through the eyes of someone completely outside the action of the story. Other times, an author chooses to tell a story through the eyes of a character who takes part in the story. The person telling the story is the ***narrator***. The kind of narrator determines the way that you see people, actions, and situations. This is called the narrator's ***point of view***.

"OUTSIDE" NARRATOR

The "outside" narrator does not participate in the conflict of a story. In fact, the outside narrator is not a character at all. This kind of narrator is, instead, a voice relating a story from a distance. The narrator recounts the characters' experiences and may tell you about their thoughts and feelings, as if able to read their minds.

The outside narrator is used in many types of fiction. As you read the following excerpt from the fairy tale "Hansel and Gretel," notice whose voice is conveying information about the characters, their circumstances, and their environment.

Close to a large forest there lived a woodcutter with his wife and his two children. The boy was called Hansel and the girl Gretel. They were always very poor and had very little to live on. And at one time when there was famine in the land, he could no longer procure daily bread.

She knew that she would weep again when she saw the kind, tender hands folded in death; the face that had never looked save
85 with love upon her, fixed and gray and dead. But she saw beyond that bitter moment a long procession of years to come that would belong to her absolutely. And she opened and spread her arms out to them
90 in welcome.

—Kate Chopin, excerpted from "The Story of an Hour," 1892

1. What caused the husband's death?

(1) heart disease
(2) a fire in the office where he worked
(3) poison given to him by his wife
(4) old age
(5) a railroad accident

2. How does the woman find out about her husband's death?

(1) Her sister Josephine tells her.
(2) She reads about it in the newspaper.
(3) Her husband's friend Richards sends her a telegram.
(4) The family doctor sends a messenger.
(5) One of her servants comes to her room to tell her.

3. The major conflict, or clash between opposing forces, that takes place in the story is

(1) an argument between the woman and her husband
(2) the husband's fight for his life
(3) the woman's struggle to understand her true feelings
(4) friction between the woman and her family and friends
(5) a psychological battle between the woman and death

4. Which of the following statements best sums up the theme of the story?

(1) It is difficult to adjust to the loss of a loved one.
(2) There is joy to be found in even the saddest situations.
(3) The need for personal freedom is stronger than the need for love.
(4) Most people have a deep-seated fear of the unknown.
(5) Each person has a right to grieve in his or her own way.

5. It is fitting that the action takes place in the spring, a time of rebirth and hope, because this setting

(1) is needed to lighten the tone of an otherwise sad story
(2) is like the husband, who had an upbeat, sunny personality
(3) indicates that the family will help the woman recover from her loss
(4) reflects how the woman feels about life after her husband's death
(5) helps readers cope with the shocking death of the husband

6. Which of the following statements would the author of the story be most likely to agree with?

(1) Women find it harder to cope with death than men do.
(2) A wife should lead her own life and refuse to live in her husband's shadow.
(3) It takes a year or longer to get over a deep personal loss.
(4) No one knows a person better than her own family and friends.
(5) It's best to look on the bright side of life and forget about your troubles.

ANSWERS ARE ON PAGE 305.

EXERCISE 12

This selection is a complete short story that is longer than the reading selections on the GED Literature and the Arts Test. It is included here to give you an opportunity to see how writers use all the elements of fiction that you have studied.

Directions: In the following short story, Walter Mitty, the main character, has five fantasies. In each, he pretends that he is a different person. Except for the fantasies in the first and last paragraphs, the passages in which Walter Mitty fantasizes are set off at the beginning and end by three dots called an *ellipsis* (. . .). These events occur in his imagination. The other paragraphs tell what really is happening in the story. Carefully read the short story and answer the questions that follow.

The Secret Life of Walter Mitty

"We're going through!" The Commander's voice was like thin ice breaking. He wore his full-dress uniform, with the heavily braided white cap pulled down rakishly over one cold gray eye. "We can't make it, sir. It's spoiling for a hurricane, if you ask me." "I'm not asking you, Lieutenant
5　Berg," said the Commander. "Throw on the power lights! Rev her up to 8,500! We're going through!" The pounding of the cylinders increased: ta-pocketa-pocketa-pocketa-*pocketa-pocketa*. The Commander stared at the ice forming on the pilot window. He walked over and twisted a row of complicated dials. "Switch on No. 8 auxiliary!" he shouted. "Switch on No. 8
10　auxiliary!" repeated Lieutenant Berg. "Full strength in No. 3 turret!" The crew, bending to their various tasks in the huge, hurtling eight-engined Navy hydroplane, looked at each other and grinned. "The Old Man'll get us through," they said to one another. "The Old Man ain't afraid of Hell!" . . .

"Not so fast! You're driving too fast!" said Mrs. Mitty. "What are you
15　driving so fast for?"

"Hmm?" said Walter Mitty. He looked at his wife, in the seat beside him, with shocked astonishment. She seemed grossly unfamiliar, like a strange woman who had yelled at him in a crowd. "You were up to fifty-five," she said. "You know I don't like to go more than forty. You were
20　up to fifty-five." Walter Mitty drove on toward Waterbury in silence, the roaring of the SN202 through the worst storm in twenty years of Navy flying fading in the remote, intimate airways of his mind.

"You're tensed up again," said Mrs. Mitty. "It's one of your days. I wish you'd let Dr. Renshaw look you over."

25　Walter Mitty stopped the car in front of the building where his wife went to have her hair done. "Remember to get those overshoes while I'm having my hair done," she said. "I don't need overshoes," said Mitty. She put her mirror back into her bag. "We've been all through that," she said, getting out of the car. "You're not a young man any longer." He raced the
30　engine a little. "Why don't you wear your gloves? Have you lost your gloves?" Walter Mitty reached in a pocket and brought out the gloves. He put them on, but after she had turned and gone into the building and he had driven on to a red light, he took them off again. "Pick it up, brother!" snapped a cop as the light changed, and Mitty hastily pulled on his gloves

35 and lurched ahead. He drove around the streets aimlessly for a time, and
then he drove past the hospital on his way to the parking lot.

. . . "It's the millionaire banker, Wellington McMillan," said the pretty
nurse. "Yes?" said Walter Mitty, removing his gloves slowly. "Who has the
case?" "Dr. Renshaw and Dr. Benbow, but there are two specialists here,
40 Dr. Remington from New York and Mr. Pritchard-Mitford from London. He
flew over." A door opened down a long, cool corridor and Dr. Renshaw
came out. He looked distraught and haggard. "Hello, Mitty," he said. "We're
having the devil's own time with McMillan, the millionaire banker and close
personal friend of Roosevelt. Obstreosis of the ductal tract. Tertiary. Wish
45 you'd take a look at him." "Glad to," said Mitty.

In the operating room there were whispered introductions: "Dr.
Remington, Dr. Mitty. Mr. Pritchard-Mitford, Dr. Mitty." "I've read your book
on streptothricosis," said Pritchard-Mitford, shaking hands. "A brilliant
performance, sir." "Thank you," said Walter Mitty. "Didn't know you were in
50 the States, Mitty," grumbled Remington. "Coals to Newcastle, bringing
Mitford and me up here for a tertiary." "You are very kind," said Mitty. A
huge, complicated machine, connected to the operating table, with many
tubes and wires, began at this moment to go pocketa-pocketa-pocketa.
"The new anesthetizer is giving way!" shouted an interne. "There is no one
55 in the East who knows how to fix it!" "Quiet, man!" said Mitty, in a low, cool
voice. He sprang to the machine, which was now going pocketa-pocketa-
queep-pocketa-queep. He began fingering delicately a row of glistening
dials. "Give me a fountain pen!" he snapped. Someone handed him a
fountain pen. He pulled a faulty piston out of the machine and inserted the
60 pen in its place. "That will hold for ten minutes," he said. "Get on with the
operation." A nurse hurried over and whispered to Renshaw, and Mitty saw
the man turn pale. "Coreopsis has set in," said Renshaw nervously. "If you
would take over, Mitty?" Mitty looked at him and at the craven figure of
Benbow, who drank, and at the grave, uncertain faces of the two great
65 specialists. "If you wish," he said. They slipped a white gown on him; he
adjusted a mask and drew on thin gloves; nurses handed him shining . . .

"Back it up, Mac! Look out for that Buick!" Walter Mitty jammed on the
brakes. "Wrong lane, Mac," said the parking-lot attendant, looking at Mitty
closely. "Gee. Yeh," muttered Mitty. He began cautiously to back out of the
70 lane marked "Exit Only." "Leave her sit there," said the attendant. "I'll put
her away." Mitty got out of the car. "Hey, better leave the key." "Oh," said
Mitty, handing the man the ignition key. The attendant vaulted into the car,
backed it up with insolent skill, and put it where it belonged.

They're so damn cocky, thought Walter Mitty, walking along Main
75 Street; they think they know everything. Once he had tried to take his
chains off, outside New Milford, and he had got them wound around the
axles. A man had had to come out in a wrecking car and unwind them, a
young, grinning garageman. Since then Mrs. Mitty always made him drive to
a garage to have the chains taken off. The next time, he thought, I'll wear
80 my right arm in a sling; they won't grin at me then. I'll have my right arm in
a sling and they'll see I couldn't possibly take the chains off myself. He
kicked at the slush on the sidewalk. "Overshoes," he said to himself, and he
began looking for a shoe store.

When he came out into the street again, with the overshoes in a box
85 under his arm, Walter Mitty began to wonder what the other thing was his
wife had told him to get. She had told him, twice, before they set out from
their house for Waterbury. In a way he hated these weekly trips to town—he
was always getting something wrong. Kleenex, he thought, Squibb's, razor
blades? No. Toothpaste, toothbrush, bicarbonate, carborundum, initiative
90 and referendum? He gave it up. But she would remember it. "Where's the
what's-its-name?" she would ask. "Don't tell me you forgot the what's-its-
name." A newsboy went by shouting something about the Waterbury trial.

. . . "Perhaps this will refresh your memory." The District Attorney
suddenly thrust a heavy automatic at the quiet figure on the witness stand.
95 "Have you ever seen this before?" Walter Mitty took the gun and examined
it expertly. "This is my Webley-Vickers 50.80," he said calmly. An excited
buzz ran around the courtroom. The Judge rapped for order. "You are a
crack shot with any sort of firearms, I believe?" said the District Attorney,
insinuatingly. "Objection!" shouted Mitty's attorney. "We have shown that
100 the defendant could not have fired the shot. We have shown that he wore
his right arm in a sling on the night of the fourteenth of July." Walter Mitty
raised his hand briefly and the bickering attorneys were stilled. "With any
known make of gun," he said evenly, "I could have killed Gregory Fitzhurst
at three hundred feet *with my left hand*." Pandemonium broke loose in the
105 courtroom. A woman's scream rose above the bedlam and suddenly a
lovely, dark-haired girl was in Walter Mitty's arms. The District Attorney
struck at her savagely. Without rising from his chair, Mitty let the man have
it on the point of the chin. "You miserable cur!" . . .

"Puppy biscuit," said Walter Mitty. He stopped walking and the
110 buildings of Waterbury rose up out of the misty courtroom and surrounded
him again. A woman who was passing laughed. "He said 'Puppy biscuit,'"
she said to her companion. "That man said 'Puppy biscuit' to himself."
Walter Mitty hurried on. He went into an A. & P., not the first one he came
to but a smaller one farther up the street. "I want some biscuit for small,
115 young dogs," he said to the clerk. "Any special brand, sir?" The greatest
pistol shot in the world thought a moment. "It says 'Puppies Bark for It' on
the box," said Walter Mitty.

His wife would be through at the hairdresser's in fifteen minutes, Mitty
saw in looking at his watch, unless they had trouble drying it; sometimes
120 they had trouble drying it. She didn't like to get to the hotel first; she would
want him to be there waiting for her as usual. He found a big leather chair
in the lobby, facing a window, and he put the overshoes and the puppy
biscuit on the floor beside it. He picked up an old copy of *Liberty* and sank
down into the chair. "Can Germany Conquer the World Through the Air?"
125 Walter Mitty looked at the pictures of bombing planes and of ruined streets.

. . . "The cannonading has got the wind up in young Raleigh, sir," said
the sergeant. Captain Mitty looked up at him through touseled hair. "Get
him to bed," he said wearily. "With the others. I'll fly alone." "But you can't,
sir," said the sergeant anxiously. "It takes two men to handle that bomber
130 and the Archies are pounding hell out of the air. Von Richtman's circus is
between here and Saulier." "Somebody's got to get that ammunition dump,"

said Mitty. "I'm going over. Spot of brandy?" He poured a drink for the sergeant and one for himself. War thundered and whined around the dugout and battered at the door. There was a rending of wood and splinters flew

135 through the room. "A bit of a near thing," said Captain Mitty carelessly. "The box barrage is closing in," said the sergeant. "We only live once, Sergeant," said Mitty, with his faint, fleeting smile. "Or do we?" He poured another brandy and tossed it off. "I never seen a man could hold his brandy like you, sir," said the sergeant. "Begging your pardon, sir." Captain Mitty

140 stood up and strapped on his huge Webley-Vickers automatic. "It's forty kilometers through hell, sir," said the sergeant. Mitty finished one last brandy. "After all," he said softly, "what isn't?" The pounding of the cannon increased; there was the rat-tat-tatting of machine guns, and from somewhere came the menacing pocketa-pocketa-pocketa of the new flame-

145 throwers. Walter Mitty walked to the door of the dugout humming "Auprès de Ma Blonde." He turned and waved to the sergeant. "Cheerio!" he said . . .

Something struck his shoulder. "I've been looking all over this hotel for you," said Mrs. Mitty. "Why do you have to hide in this old chair? How did you expect me to find you?" "Things close in," said Walter Mitty vaguely.

150 "What?" Mrs. Mitty said. "Did you get the what's-its-name? The puppy biscuit? What's in that box?" "Overshoes," said Mitty. "Couldn't you have put them on in the store?" "I was thinking," said Walter Mitty. "Does it ever occur to you that I am sometimes thinking?" She looked at him. "I'm going to take your temperature when I get you home," she said.

155 They went out through the revolving doors that made a faintly derisive whistling sound when you pushed them. It was two blocks to the parking lot. At the drugstore on the corner she said, "Wait here for me. I forgot something. I won't be a minute." She was more than a minute. Walter Mitty lighted a cigarette. It began to rain, rain with sleet in it. He stood up against

160 the wall of the drugstore, smoking. . . . He put his shoulders back and his heels together. "To hell with the handkerchief," said Walter Mitty scornfully. He took one last drag on his cigarette and snapped it away. Then, with that faint, fleeting smile playing about his lips, he faced the firing squad; erect and motionless, proud and disdainful, Walter Mitty the Undefeated,

165 inscrutable to the last.

—James Thurber

1. Mr. and Mrs. Mitty are driving to what city? _____

2. Mr. Mitty stops at several places during his trip to the city. These places are listed below in jumbled order. Number them according to the sequence in which they are mentioned in the story.

_____ parking lot

_____ hotel lobby

_____ beauty parlor

_____ shoe store

_____ A & P grocery store

3. Walter Mitty's fantasies are influenced by his real-life experiences. The first example in the chart below illustrates the cause-and-effect relationship between an actual incident (the cause) and the daydream (the effect). Using the example as a model, identify the fantasy that stems from the real situation.

Real Incident (the cause)	Fantasy (the effect)
Speeding in his car	Character: Commander of a navy plane Situation: Flying the plane during a dangerous storm
Driving past a hospital on his way to the parking lot	Character: _____ Situation: _____ _____
A newspaper boy shouting about the Waterbury trial	Character: _____ Situation: _____ _____
Reading a magazine article entitled "Can Germany Conquer the World Through the Air?"	Character: _____ Situation: _____ _____

4. From Mrs. Mitty's conversations with her husband, you can infer that she is bossy and critical. Identify three lines of dialogue that support this inference.

_____

_____

_____

5. In his fantasies, Walter Mitty imagines himself as

    (1) wealthy and selfish
    (2) modest and shy
    (3) forgetful and foolish
    (4) strong and courageous
    (5) tense and fearful

6. One of the major themes expressed in the story is that

    (1) adults who fantasize are emotionally disturbed
    (2) doctors know how to handle pressure
    (3) husbands resent their wives
    (4) parking lot attendants are rude
    (5) people daydream to escape the dull routine of life

7. The subject of this short story would be best suited for which of the following television shows? A

    (1) soap opera
    (2) situation comedy
    (3) science fiction series
    (4) news program
    (5) courtroom drama

ANSWERS ARE ON PAGE 305.

WRITING ACTIVITY 7

Like Walter Mitty, most people daydream. On a separate sheet of paper, describe a fantasy that you have had. Your description should include the answers to the following questions:

- What is the imaginary situation?

- Where and when does the fantasy occur?

- What role do you play in the fantasy?

ANSWERS WILL VARY.

GED Practice

PROSE FICTION

Read each passage below and choose the best answer to each question that follows.

Questions 1–7 refer to the following excerpt from a novel.

HOW DOES A CROWD BEHAVE AT THE PREMIERE OF A HOLLYWOOD MOVIE?

Although it was still several hours before the celebrities would arrive, thousands of people had already gathered. They stood facing the theatre with their backs toward
5 the gutter in a thick line hundreds of feet long. A big squad of policemen was trying to keep a lane open between the front rank of the crowd and the façade of the theatre.

Tod entered the lane while the
10 policeman guarding it was busy with a woman whose parcel had torn open, dropping oranges all over the place. Another policeman shouted for him to get the hell across the street, but he took a chance and
15 kept going. They had enough to do without chasing him. He noticed how worried they looked and how careful they tried to be. If they had to arrest someone, they joked good-naturedly with the culprit, making light
20 of it until they got him around the corner, then they whaled him with their clubs. Only so long as the man was actually part of the crowd did they have to be gentle.

Tod had walked only a short distance
25 along the narrow lane when he began to get frightened. People shouted, commenting on his hat, his carriage, and his clothing. There was a continuous roar of catcalls, laughter and yells, pierced occasionally by a scream.

30 The scream was usually followed by a sudden movement in the dense mass and part of it would surge forward wherever the police line was weakest. As soon as that part was rammed back, the bulge would pop
35 out somewhere else.

The police force would have to be doubled when the stars started to arrive. At the sight of their heroes and heroines, the crowd would turn demoniac. Some little
40 gesture, either too pleasing or too offensive, would start it moving and then nothing but machine guns would stop it. Individually the purpose of its members might simply to be to get a souvenir, but collectively it would
45 grab and rend.

A young man with a portable microphone was describing the scene. His rapid, hysterical voice was like that of a revivalist preacher whipping his
50 congregation toward the ecstasy of fits.

"What a crowd folks! What a crowd! There must be ten thousand excited, screaming fans outside Kahn's Persian tonight. The police can't hold them. Here,
55 listen to them roar."

—Nathanael West, excerpted from
The Day of the Locust, 1939

1. How did the police treat an arrested person after he was separated from the crowd?

   (1) carefully
   (2) gently
   (3) good-naturedly
   (4) jokingly
   (5) violently

2. The purpose of the second and third paragraphs is to describe

   (1) the movement of the crowd
   (2) Tod's observations of the scene
   (3) the personalities of the policemen
   (4) the effects of a woman dropping oranges
   (5) the physical appearance of individuals within the crowd

3. According to the passage, which of the following words best describes Tod's feeling toward the crowd?

   (1) excitement
   (2) surprise
   (3) resentment
   (4) fright
   (5) admiration

4. "His rapid, hysterical voice was like that of a revivalist preacher whipping his congregation toward the ecstasy of fits" (lines 47–50).
   The author uses this comparison to show that the man with the microphone

   (1) has strong religious convictions
   (2) is rehearsing the role of a preacher
   (3) enjoys listening to sermons
   (4) speaks in an agitated and manipulative manner
   (5) wants to lead a congregation

5. In this excerpt, who is telling the story?

   (1) Tod
   (2) an outside narrator
   (3) the man with the microphone
   (4) a policeman
   (5) a movie star

6. Which statement best expresses the theme of the passage?

   (1) When controlling a crowd, police should practice nonviolence.
   (2) When a crowd turns into a mob, people lose their individual identities.
   (3) Hollywood celebrities like their fans to show devotion.
   (4) Law and order at outdoor events should be strictly enforced.
   (5) Cities should put extra police on duty when large crowds gather.

7. The scene described in this passage also portrays the way crowds sometimes behave at

   (1) a zoo
   (2) a rock concert
   (3) an amusement park
   (4) a religious gathering
   (5) a trade show

Questions 8–12 refer to the following excerpt from a novel.

WHAT DOES PIP NOTICE ABOUT MISS HAVISHAM?

She was dressed in rich materials—satins, and lace, and silks—all of white. Her shoes were white. And she had a long white veil dependent from her hair, and she had
5 bridal flowers in her hair, but her hair was white. Some bright jewels sparkled on her neck and on her hands, and some other jewels lay sparkling on the table. Dresses, less splendid than the dress she wore, and
10 half-packed trunks, were scattered about. She had not quite finished dressing, for she had but one shoe on—the other was on the table near her hand—her veil was but half arranged, her watch and chain were not put
15 on, and some lace for her bosom lay with those trinkets, and with her handkerchief, and gloves, and some flowers, and a Prayer-book, all confusedly heaped about the looking-glass.

20 It was not in the first few moments that I saw all these things, though I saw more of them in the first moments than might be supposed. But, I saw that everything within my view which ought to be white, had been
25 white long ago, and had lost its lustre, and was faded and yellow. I saw that the bride within the bridal dress had withered like the dress, and like the flowers, and had no brightness left but the brightness of her
30 sunken eyes. I saw that the dress had been put upon the rounded figure of a young woman, and that the figure upon which it now hung loose, had shrunk to skin and bone. . . .

35 "Who is it?" said the lady at the table.

"Pip, ma'am."

"Pip?"

"Mr. Pumblechook's boy, ma'am. Come—to play."

40 "Come nearer; let me look at you. Come close."

It was when I stood before her, avoiding her eyes, that I took note of surrounding objects in detail, and saw that her watch had
45 stopped at twenty minutes to nine, and that a clock in the room had stopped at twenty minutes to nine.

—Charles Dickens, excerpted from *Great Expectations*, 1861

8. The scene takes place in

   (1) a parlor
   (2) a living room
   (3) a bedroom
   (4) an attic
   (5) an enclosed porch

9. In this excerpt, the author reveals the character of Miss Havisham by

   (1) analyzing her relationship with Pip
   (2) summarizing events from her past
   (3) describing her physical appearance and surroundings
   (4) detailing the reasons for her behavior
   (5) presenting her opinion of herself

10. Based on lines 1–8, you can conclude that Miss Havisham is

    (1) wealthy
    (2) embarrassed
    (3) nervous
    (4) beautiful
    (5) greedy

11. The descriptive details in lines 23–34 suggest an atmosphere of

    (1) decay
    (2) disappointment
    (3) loneliness
    (4) frustration
    (5) desperation

12. From whose point of view is the story told?

    (1) the author's
    (2) Miss Havisham's
    (3) a bride's
    (4) Mr. Pumblechook's
    (5) Pip's

Questions 13–18 refer to the following excerpt from an essay.

WHAT DOES AN AUTHOR SAY ABOUT WRITING?

As I wrote I followed, almost unconsciously, many principles of the novel which my reading of the novels of other writers had made me feel were necessary
5 for the building of a well-constructed book. For the most part the novel is rendered in the present; I wanted the reader to feel that Bigger's story was happening *now*, like a play upon the stage or a movie unfolding
10 upon the screen. Action follows action, as in a prize fight. Wherever possible, I told of Bigger's life in close-up, slow-motion, giving the feel of the grain in the passing of time. I had long had the feeling that this was the
15 best way to "enclose" the reader's mind in a new world, to blot out all reality except that which I was giving him.

Then again, as much as I could, I restricted the novel to what Bigger saw and
20 felt, to the limits of his feeling and thoughts, even when I was conveying *more* than that to the reader. I had the notion that such a manner of rendering made for a sharper effect, a more pointed sense of the
25 character, his peculiar type of being and consciousness. Throughout there is but one point of view: Bigger's. This, too, I felt, made for a richer illusion of reality.

I kept out of the story as much as
30 possible, for I wanted the reader to feel that there was nothing between him and Bigger; that the story was a special *première* given in his own private theater.

I kept the scenes long, made as much
35 happen within a short space of time as possible; all of which, I felt, made for greater density and richness of effect.

In a like manner I tried to keep a unified sense of background throughout the story;
40 the background would change, of course, but I tried to keep before the eyes of the reader at all times the forces and elements against which Bigger was striving.

—Richard Wright, excerpted from "How Bigger Was Born," the introduction to *Native Son*, 1940

13. How does Bigger's story resemble a prizefight?

(1) Action follows action in the novel.
(2) Bigger constantly faces conflicts.
(3) Bigger often resorts to physical violence.
(4) Bigger is in a win-lose situation.
(5) Bigger competes with other characters.

14. From whose point of view is the novel told?

(1) an outside narrator's
(2) another character's
(3) Bigger's
(4) a spectator's
(5) a movie director's

15. The author's approach to writing is

(1) disorganized
(2) inflexible
(3) deliberate
(4) relaxed
(5) illogical

16. The author wants the reader to feel that "the story was a special *première* given in his own private theater" (lines 32–33) so that the reader can

(1) pretend he owns his own playhouse
(2) feel that he experiences Bigger's life
(3) evaluate the story like a critic
(4) know what it's like to be important
(5) enjoy the novel in privacy

17. Which of the following phrases best sums up the content of the excerpt?

(1) similarities between plays and novels
(2) approaches to reading a novel
(3) techniques of novel writing
(4) influences of movies on novel writing
(5) methods for analyzing character

18. If Bigger were real rather than fictional, which of the following writers would be most likely to tell his story? A

(1) poet
(2) movie reviewer
(3) journalist
(4) songwriter
(5) playwright

ANSWERS ARE ON PAGE 305.

Edna St. Vincent Millay was a leading poet of the "lost generation" of the 1920s. Her poetry continues to move readers today.

6 Poetry

All writing has a purpose: to communicate facts, observations, opinions, or emotions. For instance, the purpose of newspaper articles is to convey facts about daily events. The journalist's responsibility is to report a truthful and precise account of an incident.

On September 16, 1963, a dynamite explosion in the Sixteenth Street Baptist Church in Birmingham, Alabama, killed four young African-American girls. The following excerpt from a news story highlights important details about the incident:

> The four girls killed in the blast had just heard Mrs. Ella C. Demand, their teacher, complete the Sunday School lesson for the day. The subject was "The Love That Forgives."
>
> During the period between the class and an assembly in the main auditorium, they went to the women's lounge in the basement at the northeast corner of the church.
>
> The blast occurred at about 10:25 A.M. . . .
>
> Church members said they found the girls huddled together beneath a pile of masonry debris.
>
> —Excerpted from "Four Negro Girls Killed in Birmingham Church Bombing," *New York Times*

Dudley Randall, a poet, told the story of the bombing in a poem. The events he chose to include in the story are quite different from those reported in the news story. He relates an imaginary conversation between a mother and her daughter, one of the four victims. In his interpretation, the mother mistakenly assumes that going to church is safer than marching in a civil rights demonstration. The poet, unlike the journalist, is not obliged to report the actual circumstances of an event. Often, poets are more interested in conveying emotional truths than in reporting facts. The poem "Ballad of Birmingham" illustrates how poets see real-life experiences in original and imaginative ways.

As you study the poem, compare and contrast its content, style, and structure with the newspaper story of the bombing. The comments in the right-hand column will help to guide your reading.

The Poem	*Comments on Structure and Content*
Ballad of Birmingham	Title of the poem
(On the Bombing of a Church in Birmingham, Alabama, 1963)	Poet's reason for writing the poem
"Mother dear, may I go downtown Instead of out to play, And march the streets of Birmingham In a Freedom March today?"	*Stanza 1:* Daughter's spoken words Daughter asks to attend the civil rights demonstration.
5 "No, baby, no, you may not go, For the dogs are fierce and wild, And clubs and hoses, guns and jail Aren't good for a little child."	*Stanza 2:* Mother's spoken words Mother gives reasons for her refusal.
"But, mother, I won't be alone. 10 Other children will go with me, And march the streets of Birmingham To make our country free."	*Stanza 3:* Daughter's spoken words Daughter tries to change her mother's mind.
"No, baby, no, you may not go, For I fear those guns will fire. 15 But you may go to church instead And sing in the children's choir."	*Stanza 4:* Mother's spoken words Mother again denies her daughter's request.
She has combed and brushed her night-dark hair, And bathed rose petal sweet, And drawn white gloves on her small brown hands 20 And white shoes on her feet.	*Stanza 5:* Daughter's physical appearance Mother dresses her daughter.
The mother smiled to know her child Was in the sacred place, But that smile was the last smile To come upon her face.	*Stanza 6:* Mother's feelings Hints suggest that a tragic event will occur.
25 For when she heard the explosion, Her eyes grew wet and wild. She raced through the streets of Birmingham Calling for her child.	*Stanza 7:* Mother's response to the explosion Mother looks for her daughter.
She clawed through bits of glass and brick, 30 Then lifted out a shoe. "O here's the shoe my baby wore, But, baby, where are you?"	*Stanza 8:* Mother's actions and spoken words Mother discovers her daughter is dead.

Compare some of the characteristics of the newspaper article and the poem. The following chart analyzes the major differences.

Characteristics	Newspaper Article	"Ballad of Birmingham"
Visual Appearance and Arrangement of Words on the Page	Groups sentences into paragraphs	Divides sentences into lines. Four lines are clustered together to form a unit called a *stanza*.
Sound of the Words	Words in the newspaper article don't rhyme.	In the second and fourth lines of each stanza, the last word rhymes. The rhyming words produce a musical effect.
Author's Purpose	To inform the reader	To affect the reader emotionally
Style of Language	Simple, direct statements Examples: "The blast occurred at about 10:25 A.M." "Church members said they found the girls huddled together beneath a pile of masonry debris."	Descriptive language that creates vivid images Examples: "Her eyes grew wet and wild." "She clawed through bits of glass and brick."

CHARACTERISTICS OF POETRY

The observations in the chart on page 165 can help you form generalizations about poetry. Here are some common characteristics of poems:

- Sentences are divided into lines. Sometimes lines are grouped into stanzas. (See example on page 164.)

- The sounds and sequence of words produce a musical effect.

- Descriptive language, both literal and figurative, creates striking images that may affect the reader emotionally.

- Like tone of voice, the tone of a poem reveals the speaker's feelings and attitudes about a subject.

- Poetry imaginatively portrays a wide range of subjects, including both serious topics and everyday experiences and observations.

EXERCISE 1

Directions: Reread "Ballad of Birmingham." Then answer the following questions.

1. The last words in the even-numbered lines of each stanza rhyme. In the spaces provided, write the eight pairs of rhyming words.

Lines 2 & 4: _____   _____

Lines 6 & 8: _____   _____

Lines 10 & 12: _____   _____

Lines 14 & 16: _____   _____

Lines 18 & 20: _____   _____

Lines 22 & 24: _____   _____

Lines 26 & 28: _____   _____

Lines 30 & 32: _____   _____

2. Write the specific line or lines from the poem that support(s) each of the following statements:

(1) The streets of Birmingham, Alabama, were dangerous.

_____

_____

_____

(2) The mother was crying.

_____

(3) The mother searched for her daughter at the church.

_____

(4) The mother found evidence that her daughter was dead.

_____

3. Read the following statements. Choose *T* if the statement is true or *F* if it is false.

T F   **(1)** The poet directly states his personal reaction to the bombing.

T F   **(2)** The poem suggests that the girl would have lived if she had attended the ''Freedom March.''

T F   **(3)** The poet reveals the mother's grief and horror.

T F   **(4)** The words and rhythm of the poem are similar to those of a song.

ANSWERS ARE ON PAGE 306.

WRITING ACTIVITY 1

Find a newspaper article that affects you emotionally. On a separate sheet of paper, write a poem about the story. Imagine the people who were involved in the incident. To make an interesting poem, add descriptive details not reported in the original article. Experiment with different ways of arranging the words on the page.

ANSWERS WILL VARY.

SUGGESTIONS FOR READING POETRY

How should you read a poem? Kenneth Koch and Kate Farrell, two modern poets, offer the following advice:

> The best way to begin is by reading the poem several times to get used to the style. After you get a sense of the whole poem, there are some things you can do to help yourself understand anything that's unclear—if anything still is unclear, which often it won't be. There may be a word or two you don't understand, or a reference to a person or a place that you're not familiar with. These you can look up in a dictionary or encyclopedia or ask someone about. There may be a sentence that's so long it's hard to follow, or a sentence that's left incomplete; words may be in an unusual order, or a sentence may be hard to see because it's divided into different lines. For these problems, just go through the poem slowly, seeing where the different sentences begin and end. If you understand part of a poem and not another part, try to use what you do understand to help you see what the rest means.

> —Excerpted from *Sleeping on the Wing*

On the following lines, write four suggestions that Koch and Farrell make for reading a poem:

1. _____

2. _____

3. _____

4. _____

Did you include some of these major points?

- Read the poem several times to get accustomed to the poet's style—the way he or she uses language.

- Look up unfamiliar words in a dictionary or an encyclopedia.

- Read the poem slowly. Notice where sentences begin and end. (Note: A period usually marks the end of a complete sentence. In some poems, the first word of each line is capitalized. Don't assume that the capitalization signals the beginning of a new sentence.)

- Apply what you already understand about part of the poem to the parts that seem more difficult.

In addition to these suggestions, here are a few more guidelines:

- Read the poem aloud. Listen to the sound and the rhythm of the words.

- Pay attention to the title. The title may provide clues about the topic and the theme of the poem.

- Identify the speaker of the poem. Like the narrator of a short story or a novel, the **speaker** represents a person's voice. The poet invents a voice to narrate the poem. If the poem uses the pronoun *I*, don't assume that *I* refers to the poet personally.

- Grasp the literal meaning of the poem—what the poet directly tells you. Infer the suggested meaning if there is one.

When you interpret poetry, you practice all the reading skills presented in the first three chapters of this textbook:

- understanding the literal meaning—the poem's directly stated main ideas and supporting details

- making inferences based on the literal meaning

- analyzing style and structure—the way a poet uses language and arranges content

In some poems, you also will find the same kinds of elements you find in fiction—for example, setting, plot, characterization, and dialogue.

EXERCISE 2

Directions: In the poem below, Janet Campbell Hale, a Native American poet, writes about a person, a place, and an event. Read the poem and answer the questions that follow.

       I lay my hand
       Upon
       The coldness of the smooth
       White stone,
5   My fingers touch the words,
       I read again:
       My father's name,
       Date of birth,
       Date of death,
10   Veteran of
       World War I.

       "This is your
       Grandfather's grave,"
       I tell my children,
15   Wishing I could tell them,
       That they would understand,
       That the man
       Who was my father,
       Was of that first generation,
20   Born on old land
       Newly made reservation,
       That at twelve,
       He went to Mission School,
       To learn to wear shoes,
25   To eat with knife and fork,
       To pray to the Catholic God,
       To painfully
       Learn English words,
       English meanings,
30   White ways of thinking,
       English words,
       To speak,
       To think,
       To write,
35   English words,
       When we,
       My children
       And I
       Know no others.

                    —Excerpted from "Tribal Cemetery"

1. The poem takes place at

   (1) an Indian reservation
   (2) the Mission School
   (3) a graveyard
   (4) a funeral parlor
   (5) a Catholic church

2. The speaker (the person telling the story in the poem) is

   (1) the father
   (2) the father's daughter
   (3) the grandchildren
   (4) a priest
   (5) a schoolteacher

3. The phrase *English words* is repeated three times (lines 28, 31, and 35) to

   (1) praise the superiority of the English language
   (2) emphasize that English was a foreign language for the father to learn
   (3) show that a knowledge of English helps people find good jobs
   (4) stress the importance of studying vocabulary, speech, and grammar
   (5) demonstrate that the father was a poor student

4. How does the daughter feel about her father?

   (1) proud
   (2) angry
   (3) disrespectful
   (4) suspicious
   (5) annoyed

5. The following inferences are based on statements in the poem. Write *V* if a statement is valid or *I* if it is invalid.

   _____ **(1)** The father was honored with medals for his bravery as a soldier.

   _____ **(2)** Beginning at the age of twelve, the father began to lose touch with his original heritage.

   _____ **(3)** The father practiced only his native religion all his life.

   _____ **(4)** The generations after the father are disconnected from their Native American roots.

   _____ **(5)** The purpose of the father's training at the Mission School was to make him conform to white American culture.

   _____ **(6)** Non-English-speaking immigrants arriving in the United States could probably identify with the father's difficulty in adapting to American society.

ANSWERS ARE ON PAGE 306.

UNDERSTANDING THE LANGUAGE OF POETRY

One of the most striking characteristics of poetry is its attention to language. Poetic language often appeals to the senses—sights, sounds, odors, textures, and tastes.

Poets use both literal statements and figures of speech to express sensations and ideas. In this section, you will learn how poets describe their perceptions through literal and figurative language.

LITERAL DESCRIPTIONS

Literal descriptions can help you visualize the physical appearance of a person, place, or thing. The central purpose of purely descriptive poetry is to help you "see" a detailed image.

Use your imagination to picture the man described in the following poem:

The Runner

On a flat road runs the well-train'd runner;
He is lean and sinewy, with muscular legs;
He is thinly clothed—he leans forward as he runs,
With lightly closed fists, and arms partially rais'd.

—Walt Whitman

Can you see a clear image of the runner? Reread the poem and write the specific words or phrases that answer these questions:

1. Where is the man running? _____

2. What words describe the runner's build? _____

_____

3. How is the runner dressed? _____

4. What pose does he strike as he runs? _____

_____

Here are the correct responses:

1. "on a flat road"
2. "lean"; "sinewy"; "muscular legs"
3. "thinly clothed"
4. "leans forward"; "lightly closed fists"; "arms partially rais'd"

The total effect of these descriptive details creates a vivid portrait of a runner. The words produce an image as distinct as a snapshot.

WRITING ACTIVITY 2

Study the photograph below. On a separate sheet of paper, write a short poem in which you re-create the image of the athlete through descriptive words and phrases. Use Walt Whitman's poem "The Runner" as a model.

ANSWERS WILL VARY.

MORE PRACTICE WITH DESCRIPTIONS

In the preceding poem, Walt Whitman directly shows you what the runner looks like. He offers no comments about the runner's personality. However, you can infer that the poet admires the runner's physical appearance and athletic ability.

As you already know from reading fiction, a character's physical appearance and actions often reveal his or her personality. In the next excerpt, a stanza from the poem "Kindergarten," the speaker describes a school principal. Circle the words and phrases that create a picture in your mind.

> The principal had a long black whip
> studded through with razor blades
> and nine lashes on it.
> The principal wore a black suit
> and smoked Pall Malls
> and wrote bad notes to your father.
>
> —Ronald Rogers

You can infer that the speaker of the poem fears the principal. Why? Write the descriptive details that support this inference.

_____

_____

_____

_____

_____

_____

The first three lines and the last line suggest the speaker's fearful attitude. The detailed description of the principal's "long black whip / studded through with razor blades / and nine lashes on it" presents a threatening image. The principal also "wrote bad notes to your father"—another method he apparently used to instill fear. The literal descriptions in the poem provide you with clues about the principal's character.

FORMAT OF SCRIPTS

The excerpt from the play *Of Mice and Men* illustrates how drama tells a story in script form. This section will discuss the format of a script in more detail. Your ability to read and interpret a play will improve once you recognize the distinctive features of a script.

ACTS AND SCENES: STRUCTURING THE PLOT

Long plays are organized into major sections called **acts**. Sometimes acts are divided into **scenes**—specific episodes from the story set in one place and occurring during a fixed time period. For example, here is the organization of Dr. Endesha Ida Mae Holland's play *From the Mississippi Delta*.

Scenes

Act 1

Scene 1	Memories
Scene 2	Ain't Baby
Scene 3	Calm, Balmy Days
Scene 4	Second Doctor Lady
Scene 5	The Delta Queen

Intermission

Act II

Scene 6	The Water Meter
Scene 7	The Whole Town's Talking
Scene 8	The Funeral
Scene 9	From the Mississippi Delta
Scene 10	A Permit to Parade
Scene 11	Letter to Alice Walker: Request From the Mississippi Delta

When you pay attention to the shifts in acts and scenes, you may get clues about how the plot of the play is structured. Furthermore, you also may get clues about the events or scenes that are about to unfold.

A CAST LIST: INTRODUCING THE CHARACTERS

The first page of most scripts lists the characters who perform in the play. As you will notice in the example that follows, the cast list includes the following information about the main characters:

1. name

2. age

3. occupation

4. physical description or personality traits

Cast

NOLA BARNES is thirty. She is a single mother who divides her time between her son and her career as a social worker. Proud and determined, she commands respect from those around her.

SAM MILLER, thirty-four, is Nola's ex-husband. A star athlete in high school, Sam relies too much on his physical strength and appearance to impress people. He is a steelworker who would like to spend more time with Nola and David.

DAVID, Nola's eleven-year-old son, is thinner and smaller than his classmates. He is working to overcome a learning disability that has slowed his progress in school. He is a loner who shares his feelings more with his tutor at school than with his father.

DWIGHT PARKS, David's tutor, is twenty-eight. He laughs easily, is a good listener, and cares more about his students than he admits. He has never met Nola, but when she comes to pick up David, Dwight watches for her by the window.

JUAN MORALES lives in Nola's building. He is seventeen and has been arrested several times for petty theft and trespassing. He has a deep scar on his chin and looks out at the world through black, expressionless eyes.

BEATRICE LUIS, Juan's grandmother, has taken care of Juan since he was a child. Now in declining health, she worries about her grandson and would like to ask Nola for help.

LUCITA
ESMERALDA
LU-KEE   } Nola and David's neighbors
JOE
EXTRAS

STAGE DIRECTIONS: ESTABLISHING THE SETTING

As you have already learned, playwrights use stage directions to indicate a character's tone of voice, feelings, facial expressions, gestures, and actions. Stage directions also explain the setting—where and when the action takes place.

Terms such as **stage right**, **stage left**, and **down right** inform the actors of where events should take place onstage. The **wing** refers to the area on either side of the stage that is not visible to the audience.

Stage directions are given for the benefit of the actors, who face the audience from the stage. Therefore, action which occurs *stage right*—to the actors' right as they face the audience—takes place on the audience's left.

The following excerpt from Ariel Dorfman's *Death and the Maiden* shows how the setting should appear on the stage. As you read the stage directions, try to picture in your mind what this setting looks like. Notice the arrangement of furniture, windows, and doors and the stage directions for sound. Remember that the actors will perform their roles in this imaginary place.

Scene 1
Sound of the sea. After midnight.

The Escobar's beach house. A terrace and an ample living/dining room where dinner is laid out on a table with two chairs. On a sideboard is a cassette recorder and a lamp. Window walls between the terrace and the front room, with curtains blowing in the wind. A door from the terrace leading to a bedroom. Paulina Salas is seated in a chair on the terrace, as if she were drinking in the light of the moon. The sound of a faraway car can be heard. She hurriedly stands up, goes to the other room, looks out the window. The car brakes, its motor still running, the lights blasting her. She goes to the sideboard, takes out a gun, stops when the motor is turned off and she hears Gerardo's voice.

WRITING ACTIVITY 2

Imagine a room in your house or apartment as the setting for a play. Using the preceding example as a model, write a paragraph or two of stage directions explaining the physical appearance of the room. Describe the furniture and how it is arranged. Also include noticeable features of the room—the size, the condition, the color of the walls and floor, etc. Use a separate sheet of paper for this description.

ANSWERS WILL VARY.

DIALOGUE: REVEALING CHARACTER AND ADVANCING PLOT

A script consists mainly of dialogue—conversations among the characters. Dramatic dialogue, however, differs from everyday conversations with people. The playwright carefully chooses dialogue that reveals character and advances the plot. The action progresses as the characters recite their lines and participate in the events of the story. When you read a play, focus on interpreting the characters' spoken words in the context of the dramatic situation. Here are some other suggestions for reading the dialogue in a script:

1. Notice the punctuation. Playwrights sometimes use a dash (—) or an ellipsis (. . .) to indicate pauses or interruptions in the characters' speech.

2. Study the stage directions printed before and after the characters' dialogue. Look for clues that explain how the characters deliver their lines. Descriptions of voice, attitude, or actions heighten the meaning of the spoken words.

Apply these suggestions as you read the dialogue between two World War I veterans—Harold and Kenner:

HAROLD: I want to *remember*—the *good* things.

KENNER: Like being over there. Scared to death. Watching guys screamin' and bleeding to death.

HAROLD: I wasn't scared . . . not like you tell it.

KENNER: Damn . . . everybody was. Didn't you ever wake up in sweats and shivers? I used to put my blanket in my mouth and . . .

HAROLD: [*shakes his head, no.*]

KENNER: Well . . . I was scared. Everybody was.

HAROLD: [*softly*] That's a lie.

—Excerpted from the televison adaptation of "Soldier's Home"
by Ernest Hemingway (screenplay by Robert Geller)

The dash (—) and the ellipsis (. . .) show pauses or interruptions in speech. How does Harold speak when he says, "That's a lie"? If you said *softly*, you correctly recognized how the stage directions corresponded to Harold's statement.

The plot of "Soldier's Home" recounts how Harold Krebs, the main character, adjusts to civilian life following his combat experience overseas. The preceding dialogue contributes to the story's development. Harold's conversation reveals his feelings about fighting in the war. You can infer that he is still affected by his wartime memories.

═ GED Practice ═
EXERCISE 2

Read the excerpt below from *The Odd Couple* and answer the questions that follow.

CAN THIS FRIENDSHIP BE SAVED?

FELIX: What's wrong? [*Crosses back to tray, puts down glasses, etc.*]

OSCAR: There's something wrong with this system, that's what's wrong. I don't
5 think that two single men living alone in a big eight-room apartment should have a cleaner house than my mother.

FELIX: [*Gets rest of dishes, glasses and
10 coasters from table.*] What are you talking about? I'm just going to put the dishes in the sink. You want me to leave them here all night?

OSCAR: [*Takes his glass which FELIX has
15 put on tray and crosses to bar for refill.*] I don't care if you take them to bed with you. You can play Mr. Clean all you want. But don't make *me* feel guilty.

20 FELIX: [*Takes tray into kitchen, leaving swinging door open.*] I'm not asking you to do it, Oscar. You don't have to clean up.

OSCAR: [*Moves up to door.*] *That's* why
25 you make me feel guilty. You're always in my bathroom hanging up my towels. . . . Whenever I smoke you follow me around with an ashtray. . . . Last night I found
30 you washing the kitchen floor shaking your head and moaning, "Footprints, footprints"! [*Paces Right.*]

FELIX: [*Comes back to the table with
35 silent butler into which he dumps the ashtrays; then wipes them carefully.*] I didn't say they were yours.

OSCAR: [*Angrily; sits Down Right in wing
40 chair.*] Well, they *were* mine, damn it. I have feet and they make prints. What do you want me to do, climb across the cabinets?

FELIX: No! I want you to walk on
45 the floor.

OSCAR: I appreciate that! I really do.

FELIX: [*Crosses to telephone table and cleans ashtray there.*] I'm just trying to keep the place livable. I
50 didn't realize I irritated you that much.

—Neil Simon, 1966

1. Where does the scene take place?

(1) a house
(2) a hotel
(3) a dormitory
(4) an apartment
(5) a bar

2. The stage directions referring to Felix show his

(1) tone of voice
(2) facial expressions
(3) actions
(4) emotions
(5) clothing

3. Oscar's tone in lines 40–41 is

(1) guilty
(2) angry
(3) comic
(4) insincere
(5) selfish

4. What does Felix do while talking with Oscar?

(1) tidies up the surroundings
(2) refills his glass of beer
(3) smokes a cigarette
(4) hangs up Oscar's towels
(5) relaxes in a wing chair

5. What causes tension between the men?

(1) They are both unmarried.
(2) They have different housekeeping habits.
(3) Oscar smokes and Felix doesn't.
(4) Oscar is overly attached to his mother.
(5) Felix wants to be a butler.

ANSWERS ARE ON PAGE 308.

STORY ELEMENTS OF DRAMA

In plays, you will find many of the story elements that were described in the chapter on prose fiction. Review the definitions of these elements as they apply to drama.

Setting: The place, the time, and the atmosphere in which dramatic situations occur. Setting in plays is conveyed by the stage directions and the characters' comments about the physical surroundings.

Plot: The series of events tracing the action of a story. The plot of a play relies almost entirely on the characters' performance—the way they immediately respond to ongoing situations. Therefore, the plot stems from the characters, whose purpose is to act out events.

Characters involved in conflicts create moments of tension in the plot. Plays usually contain scenes showing conflicts among the characters. For example, the conflict in the scene from *Of Mice and Men* (page 197) results when George discovers that Lennie has snatched a mouse and unintentionally killed it. George's initial reaction is anger; George scolds Lennie. George resolves the conflict by telling Lennie to "get a mouse that's fresh."

Characterization: The methods of revealing character—appearance, personality, and behavior. Because plays are written in script form, you learn about the characters from reading the dialogue and the stage directions. As you read, look for clues in the dialogue and stage directions that suggest character traits. Your understanding of characterization is based largely on the inferences you make.

Theme: A general statement that explains the underlying meaning of a story. As a rule, you have to read the entire play, rather than an excerpt, to determine the significance of the dramatic action. However, the dialogue in some scenes expresses beliefs or opinions about life and human behavior. The topic of conversation and the characters' statements about that topic may reveal the major or minor theme of the play.

GED Practice
EXERCISE 3

The following excerpt is from the play *Fences*. In this scene, Rose and Troy are talking to their friend, Bono. As you read the passage, try to imagine the actors saying their lines. Then answer the questions that follow.

HAVE TIMES CHANGED FOR THE BETTER?

BONO: I hear you tell it. Me and Lucille was staying down there on Logan Street. Had two rooms with the outhouse in the back. I ain't mind the outhouse none. But when that goddamn wind blow through there in the winter . . . that's what I'm talking about! To this day I wonder why in the hell I ever stayed down there for six long years. But see, I didn't know I could do no better. I thought only white folks had inside toilets and things.

ROSE: There's a lot of people don't know they can do no better than they doing now. That's just something you got to learn. A lot of folks still shop at Bella's.

TROY: Ain't nothing wrong with shopping at Bella's. She got fresh food.

ROSE: I ain't said nothing about if she got fresh food. I'm talking about what she charge. She charge ten cents more than the A&P.

TROY: The A&P ain't never done nothing for me. I spends my money where I'm treated right. I go down to Bella, say, "I need a loaf of bread, I'll pay you Friday." She give it to me. What sense that make when I got money to go and spend it somewhere else and ignore the person who done right by me? That ain't in the Bible.

ROSE: We ain't talking about what's in the Bible. What sense it make to shop there when she overcharge?

TROY: You shop where you want to. I'll do my shopping where the people been good to me.

ROSE: Well, I don't think it's right for her to overcharge. That's all I was saying.

BONO: Look here . . . I got to get on. Lucille gonna be raising all kind of hell.

TROY: Where you going, nigger? We ain't finished this pint. Come here, finish this pint.

BONO: Well, hell, I am . . . if you ever turn the bottle loose.

TROY: [*Hands him the bottle.*] The only thing I say about the A&P is I'm glad Cory got that job down there. Help him take care of his school clothes and things. Gabe done moved out and things getting tight around here. He got that job. . . . He can start to look out for himself.

ROSE: Cory done went and got recruited by a college football team.

TROY: I told that boy about that football stuff. The white man ain't gonna let him get nowhere with that football. I told him when he first come to me with it. Now you come telling me he done went and got more tied up in it. He ought to go and get recruited in how to fix cars or something where he can make a living.

ROSE: He ain't talking about making no living playing football. It's just something the boys in school do. They gonna send a recruiter by to talk to you. He'll tell you he ain't talking about making no living playing football. It's a honor to be recruited.

TROY: It ain't gonna get him nowhere. Bono'll tell you that.

CONTINUED

80 BONO: If he be like you in the sports . . . he's gonna be alright. Ain't but two men ever played baseball as good as you. That's Babe Ruth and Josh Gibson. Them's the only two men 85 ever hit more home runs than you.

TROY: What it ever get me? Ain't got a pot to piss in or a window to throw it out of.

ROSE: Times have changed since you was 90 playing baseball, Troy. That was before the war. Times have changed a lot since then.

—August Wilson, 1986

1. Which word best describes how the three characters feel toward each other?

   (1) tense
   (2) frightened
   (3) friendly
   (4) suspicious
   (5) uncomfortable

2. Troy prefers to shop at Bella's rather than the A&P because

   (1) the prices are lower at Bella's
   (2) Bella's carries fresh food
   (3) Rose prefers Bella's
   (4) Bella has been kind to him
   (5) Bella's carries a wider variety of food

3. Which word best describes Rose in this scene?

   (1) greedy
   (2) practical
   (3) emotional
   (4) sentimental
   (5) selfish

4. How do Rose and Troy feel about their son's playing on a college football team?

   (1) They are both very proud of his accomplishment.
   (2) They would prefer that he chose a different activity.
   (3) They are hiding their true feelings from each other.
   (4) They think he can make a good living playing football.
   (5) They disagree about the value of playing college football.

5. In this scene, the characters are concerned mainly about

   (1) economic survival
   (2) struggling to keep peace
   (3) racial problems in America
   (4) getting a college education
   (5) ethical values and morality

ANSWERS ARE ON PAGE 308.

CHARACTERS: PERFORMERS OF DRAMA

In drama, the characters participate in the ongoing events of the story. Their performance is the central focus of your attention. Why? Because scripts consist almost entirely of characters' dialogue and actions. The roles the characters play develop these elements of drama—plot, characterization, and theme.

Unlike prose fiction, plays usually do not have a narrator who comments on the characters and summarizes events. Instead, you directly observe the characters performing the action. You see how they respond to past or present situations. You also imaginatively "hear" their remarks about themselves or other characters.

Based on your observations, you make inferences about the characters' dramatic role in a play. Do they cause conflicts? Do they influence events? Do they make decisions that affect the outcome of the play?

You also form opinions about the characters' personalities and relationships with other people. Do they communicate honestly, or do their words disguise their true feelings? Does their dialogue show an understanding of another character's viewpoint?

In the next exercise, you will closely examine these aspects of the characters' performance:

- comments about themselves
- comments about other people
- responses to each other's comments
- reactions to events

EXERCISE 4

Directions: Read the passage below, in which Nora confronts her husband, Torvald Helmer. Then answer the questions that follow.

NORA: Sit down. This'll take some time. I have a lot to say.

HELMER: [*sitting at the table directly opposite her*] You worry me, Nora. And I don't understand you.

NORA: No, that's exactly it. You don't understand me. And I've
5 never understood you either—until tonight. No, don't interrupt. You can just listen to what I say. We're closing out accounts, Torvald.

HELMER: How do you mean that?

NORA: [*after a short pause*] Doesn't anything strike you about our
10 sitting here like this?

HELMER: What's that?

NORA: We've been married now eight years. Doesn't it occur to you that this is the first time we two, you and I, man and wife, have ever talked seriously together?

15 HELMER: What do you mean—seriously?

NORA: In eight whole years—longer even—right from our first acquaintance, we've never exchanged a serious word on any serious thing.

HELMER: You mean I should constantly go and involve you in
20 problems you couldn't possibly help me with?

NORA: I'm not talking of problems. I'm saying that we've never sat down seriously together and tried to get to the bottom of anything.

HELMER: But dearest, what good would that ever do you?

25 NORA: That's the point right there: you've never understood me. I've been wronged greatly, Torvald—first by Papa, and then by you.

HELMER: What! By us—the two people who've loved you more than anyone else?

30 NORA: [*shaking her head*] You never loved me. You've thought it fun to be in love with me, that's all.

HELMER: Nora, what a thing to say!

NORA: Yes, it's true now, Torvald. When I lived at home with Papa, he told me all his opinions, so I had the same ones too; or if
35 they were different I hid them, since he wouldn't have cared for that. He used to call me his doll-child, and he played with me the way I played with my dolls. Then I came into your house—

HELMER: How can you speak of our marriage like that?

40 NORA: [*unperturbed*] I mean, then I went from Papa's hands into yours. You arranged everything to your own taste, and so I got the same taste as you—or I pretended to; I can't remember. I guess a little of both, first one, then the other. Now when I look back, it seems as if I'd lived here like a
45 beggar—just from hand to mouth. I've lived by doing tricks for you, Torvald. But that's the way you wanted it. It's a great sin what you and Papa did to me. You're to blame that nothing's become of me.

HELMER: Nora, how unfair and ungrateful you are! Haven't you been
50 happy here?

NORA: No, never. I thought so—but I never have.

HELMER: Not—not happy!

NORA: No, only lighthearted. And you've always been so kind to me. But our home's been nothing but a playpen. I've been
55 your doll-wife here, just as at home I was Papa's doll-child. And in turn the children have been my dolls. I thought it was fun when you played with me, just as they thought it fun when I played with them. That's been our marriage, Torvald.

60 HELMER: There's some truth in what you're saying—under all the raving exaggeration. But it'll all be different after this. Playtime's over; now for the schooling.

NORA: Whose schooling—mine or the children's?

HELMER: Both yours and the children's, dearest.

65 NORA: Oh, Torvald, you're not the man to teach me to be a good wife to you.

HELMER: And you can say that?

NORA: And I—how am I equipped to bring up children?

HELMER: Nora!

70 NORA: Didn't you say a moment ago that that was no job to trust me with?

HELMER: In a flare of temper! Why fasten on that?

NORA: Yes, but you were so very right. I'm not up to the job. There's another job I have to do first. I have to try to
75 educate myself. You can't help me with that. I've got to do it alone. And that's why I'm leaving you now.

—Excerpted from *A Doll's House* by Henrik Ibsen

CONTINUED

1. Where are Nora and Helmer seated during their conversation?

_____

2. What does Nora mean by the phrase "closing out accounts" (lines 6–7)?

(1) paying the household bills
(2) transferring the savings account to another bank
(3) filing for bankruptcy
(4) discussing financial investments
(5) ending the marriage

3. What does Nora mean when she says, "I've been your doll-wife here, just as at home I was Papa's doll-child" (lines 54–55)?

(1) She has always been pretty as a doll.
(2) She has a cute and playful personality.
(3) Neither her husband nor her father has treated her like a human being.
(4) Her husband and father collect lifelike dolls.
(5) Nora toys with her father's and Helmer's affection.

4. According to this passage, what is the significance of the title _A Doll's House_?

_____

_____

_____

5. Choose _T_ if the statement is true or _F_ if it is false.

T F **(1)** Helmer discusses serious issues with Nora.

T F **(2)** Helmer is satisfied with the marriage.

T F **(3)** Nora and Helmer disagree about the definition of love.

T F **(4)** Helmer considers Nora his equal.

T F **(5)** Helmer understands his wife's point of view.

T F **(6)** Helmer has not physically abused Nora.

6. In a short paragraph, write your opinion of either Nora or Helmer. Explain your feelings about the character's behavior and role as either a wife or a husband.

_____

_____

_____

_____

_____

_____

ANSWERS ARE ON PAGE 309.

READING A COMPLETE SCENE FROM A PLAY

In this section, you will read an entire scene from a play. Unlike a shorter passage, a complete scene presents a more detailed development of character and plot.

Use the following questions as study aids for understanding the literal meanings, the suggested meanings, and the structural elements of drama:

- Where and when does the scene occur?

- What is the topic of conversation?

- What is the literal meaning of the speaker's statements?

- What is the relationship between the stage directions and the dialogue? Do the speaker's tone of voice and actions emphasize or change the literal meaning of the spoken words?

- What do other characters say in response to the first speaker? Based on these responses, can you make inferences about the relationships of the characters involved in the conversation?

- Does the dialogue show a conflict between the characters? Is the conflict resolved?

- Do the characters in the scene discuss other people? What do the characters' comments reveal about those people?

- Does the dialogue reveal the speaker's personality, behavior, or background?

- What specific incidents of plot are depicted in the scene?

- Do characters express their beliefs or opinions about life or human behavior? If so, do their comments suggest a theme—a general statement explaining the significance of the dramatic action?

EXERCISE 5

This excerpt is longer than those you'll see on the GED Literature and the Arts Test. However, when you read the entire scene, you will see how all of the elements of drama work together.

Directions: The play *Death of a Salesman* tells the story of Willy Loman, a sixty-year-old sales representative who is approaching the end of his career. In the following scene from Act II, Willy meets with his boss, Howard. Willy proposes a change in his position with the firm. Read the script and answer the questions that follow.

[*HOWARD WAGNER, thirty-six, wheels in a small typewriter table on which is a wire-recording machine and proceeds to plug it in. This is on the left forestage. . . . HOWARD is intent on threading the machine and only glances over his shoulder as WILLY appears.*]

5

WILLY: Pst! Pst!

HOWARD: Hello, Willy, come in.

WILLY: Like to have a little talk with you, Howard.

10 HOWARD: Sorry to keep you waiting. I'll be with you in a minute.

WILLY: What's that, Howard?

HOWARD: Didn't you ever see one of these? Wire recorder.

WILLY: Oh. Can we talk a minute?

15 HOWARD: Records things. Just got delivery yesterday. Been driving me crazy, the most terrific machine I ever saw in my life. I was up all night with it.

WILLY: What do you do with it?

HOWARD: I bought it for dictation, but you can do anything
20 with it. Listen to this. I had it home last night. Listen to what I picked up. The first one is my daughter. Get this. [*He flicks the switch and "Roll out the Barrel" is heard being whistled.*] Listen to that kid whistle.

25 WILLY: That is lifelike, isn't it?

HOWARD: Seven years old. Get that tone.

WILLY: Ts, ts. Like to ask a little favor if you . . .

[*The whistling breaks off, and the voice of HOWARD'S DAUGHTER is heard.*]

30 HIS DAUGHTER: "Now you, Daddy."

HOWARD: She's crazy for me! [*Again the same song is whistled.*] That's me! Ha! [*He winks.*]

WILLY: You're very good!

[*The whistling breaks off again. The machine runs silent for a moment.*]

HOWARD: Sh! Get this now, this is my son.

HIS SON: "The capital of Alabama is Montgomery; the capital of Arizona is Phoenix; the capital of Arkansas is Little Rock; the capital of California is Sacramento . . ." [*And on, and on.*]

HOWARD: [*holding up five fingers*] Five years old, Willy!

WILLY: He'll make an announcer some day!

HIS SON: [*continuing*] "The capital . . ."

HOWARD: Get that—alphabetical order! [*The machine breaks off suddenly.*] Wait a minute. The maid kicked the plug out.

WILLY: It certainly is a—

HOWARD: Sh, for God's sake!

HIS SON: "It's nine o'clock, Bulova watch time. So I have to go to sleep."

WILLY: That really is—

HOWARD: Wait a minute. The next is my wife.

[*They wait.*]

HOWARD'S VOICE: "Go on, say something." [*Pause.*] "Well, you gonna talk?"

HIS WIFE: "I can't think of anything."

HOWARD'S VOICE: "Well, talk—it's turning."

HIS WIFE: [*shyly, beaten*] "Hello." [*Silence.*] "Oh, Howard, I can't talk into this . . ."

HOWARD: [*snapping the machine off*] That was my wife.

WILLY: That is a wonderful machine. Can we—

HOWARD: I tell you, Willy, I'm gonna take my camera, and my bandsaw, and all my hobbies, and out they go. This is the most fascinating relaxation I ever found.

WILLY: I think I'll get one myself.

CONTINUED

	HOWARD:	Sure, they're only a hundred and a half. You can't do without it. Supposing you wanna hear Jack Benny, see? But you can't be at home at that hour. So you tell the maid to turn the radio on when Jack Benny comes on, and this automatically goes on with the radio . . .

70

WILLY: And when you come home you . . .

HOWARD: You can come home twelve o'clock, one o'clock, any time you like, and you get yourself a Coke and sit yourself down, throw the switch, and there's Jack Benny's program in the middle of the night!

75

WILLY: I'm definitely going to get one. Because lots of time I'm on the road, and I think to myself, what I must be missing on the radio!

80

HOWARD: Don't you have a radio in the car?

WILLY: Well, yeah, but who ever thinks of turning it on?

HOWARD: Say, aren't you supposed to be in Boston?

WILLY: That's what I want to talk to you about, Howard. You got a minute?

85

[*He draws a chair in from the wing.*]

HOWARD: What happened? What're you doing here?

WILLY: Well . . .

HOWARD: You didn't crack up again, did you?

90

WILLY: Oh, no. No . . .

HOWARD: Geez, you had me worried there for a minute. What's the trouble?

WILLY: Well, to tell you the truth, Howard, I've come to the decision that I'd rather not travel any more.

95

HOWARD: Not travel! Well, what'll you do?

WILLY: Remember, Christmas time, when you had the party here? You said you'd try to think of some spot for me here in town.

HOWARD: With us?

100

WILLY: Well, sure.

HOWARD: Oh, yeah, yeah. I remember. Well, I couldn't think of anything for you, Willy.

WILLY: I tell ya, Howard. The kids are all grown up, y'know. I don't need much any more. If I could take home—well, sixty-five dollars a week, I could swing it.

105

HOWARD: Yeah, but Willy, see I —

110 WILLY: I tell ya why, Howard. Speaking frankly and between the two of us, y'know—I'm just a little tired.

HOWARD: Oh, I could understand that, Willy. But you're a road man, Willy, and we do a road business. We've only got a half-dozen salesmen on the floor here.

115

WILLY: God knows, Howard, I never asked a favor of any man. But I was with the firm when your father used to carry you in here in his arms.

HOWARD: I know that, Willy, but—

120 WILLY: Your father came to me the day you were born and asked me what I thought of the name of Howard, may he rest in peace.

HOWARD: I appreciate that, Willy, but there just is no spot here for you. If I had a spot I'd slam you right in, but I just don't have a single, solitary spot.

125

[*He looks for his lighter. WILLY has picked it up and gives it to him. Pause.*]

WILLY: [*with increasing anger*] Howard, all I need to set my table is fifty dollars a week.

130 HOWARD: But where am I going to put you, kid?

WILLY: Look, it isn't a question of whether I can sell merchandise, is it?

HOWARD: No, but it's a business, kid, and everybody's gotta pull his own weight.

135 WILLY: [*desperately*] Just let me tell you a story, Howard—

HOWARD: 'Cause you gotta admit, business is business.

WILLY: [*angrily*] Business is definitely business, but just listen for a minute. You don't understand this. When I was a boy—eighteen, nineteen—I was
140 already on the road. And there was a question in my mind as to whether selling had a future for me. Because in those days I had a yearning to go to Alaska. See, there were three gold strikes in
145 one month in Alaska, and I felt like going out. Just for the ride, you might say.

HOWARD: [*barely interested*] Don't say.

CONTINUED

WILLY: Oh, yeah, my father lived many years in Alaska. He was an adventurous man. We've got quite a little streak of self-reliance in our family. I thought I'd go out with my older brother and try to locate him, and maybe settle in the North with the old man. And I was almost decided to go, when I met a salesman in the Parker House. His name was Dave Singleman. And he was eighty-four years old, and he'd drummed merchandise in thirty-one states. And old Dave, he'd go up to his room, y'understand, put on his green velvet slippers—I'll never forget—and pick up his phone and call the buyers, and without ever leaving his room, at the age of eighty-four, he made his living. And when I saw that, I realized that selling was the greatest career a man could want. 'Cause what could be more satisfying than to be able to go, at the age of eighty-four, into twenty or thirty different cities, and pick up a phone, and be remembered and loved and helped by so many different people? Do you know? when he died—and by the way he died the death of a salesman, in his green velvet slippers in the smoker of the New York, New Haven, and Hartford, going into Boston—when he died, hundreds of salesmen and buyers were at his funeral. Things were sad on a lotta trains for months after that. [*He stands up. HOWARD has not looked at him.*] In those days there was personality in it, Howard. There was respect, and comradeship, and gratitude in it. Today, it's all cut and dried, and there's no chance for bringing friendship to bear—or personality. You see what I mean? They don't know me any more.

HOWARD: [*moving away, to the right*] That's just the thing, Willy.

WILLY: If I had forty dollars a week—that's all I'd need. Forty dollars, Howard.

HOWARD: Kid, I can't take blood from a stone, I—

WILLY: [*desperation is on him now*] Howard, the year Al Smith was nominated, your father came to me and—

HOWARD: [*starting to go off*] I've got to see some people, kid.

WILLY: [*stopping him*] I'm talking about your father! There were promises made across this desk! You mustn't tell me you've got people to see—I put thirty-four years into this firm, Howard, and now I can't pay my insurance! You can't eat the orange and throw the peel away—a man is not a piece of fruit! [*After a pause.*] Now pay attention. Your father—in 1928 I had a big year. I averaged a hundred and seventy dollars a week in commissions.

HOWARD: [*impatiently*] Now, Willy, you never averaged—

WILLY: [*banging his hand on the desk*] I averaged a hundred and seventy dollars a week in the year of 1928! And your father came to me—or rather, I was in the office here—it was right over this desk—and he put his hand on my shoulder—

HOWARD: [*getting up*] You'll have to excuse me, Willy, I gotta see some people. Pull yourself together. [*Going out*] I'll be back in a little while.

[*On HOWARD'S exit, the light on his chair grows very bright and strange.*]

WILLY: Pull myself together! What the hell did I say to him? My God, I was yelling at him! How could I! [*WILLY breaks off, staring at the light, which occupies the chair, animating it. He approaches this chair, standing across the desk from it.*] Frank, Frank, don't you remember what you told me that time? How you put your hand on my shoulder, and Frank . . . [*He leans on the desk and as he speaks the dead man's name he accidentally switches on the recorder, and instantly—*]

HOWARD'S SON: ". . . of New York is Albany. The capital of Ohio is Cincinnati, the capital of Rhode Island is . . ." [*The recitation continues.*]

WILLY: [*leaping away with fright, shouting*] Ha! Howard! Howard! Howard!

HOWARD: [*rushing in*] What happened?

WILLY: [*pointing at the machine, which continues nasally, childishly, with the capital cities*] Shut it off! Shut it off!

HOWARD: [*pulling the plug out*] Look, Willy . . .

WILLY: [*pressing his hands to his eyes*] I gotta get myself some coffee. I'll get some coffee . . .

CONTINUED

[*WILLY starts to walk out. HOWARD stops him.*]

235 HOWARD: [*rolling up the cord*] Willy, look . . .

WILLY: I'll go to Boston.

HOWARD: Willy, you can't go to Boston for us.

WILLY: Why can't I go?

240 HOWARD: I don't want you to represent us. I've been meaning to tell you for a long time now.

WILLY: Howard, are you firing me?

HOWARD: I think you need a good long rest, Willy.

WILLY: Howard—

245 HOWARD: And when you feel better, come back, and we'll see if we can work something out.

WILLY: But I gotta earn money, Howard. I'm in no position—

HOWARD: Where are your sons? Why don't your sons give you a hand?

250 WILLY: They're working on a very big deal.

HOWARD: This is no time for false pride, Willy. You go to your sons and tell them that you're tired. You've got two great boys, haven't you?

255 WILLY: Oh, no question, no question, but in the meantime . . .

HOWARD: Then that's that, heh?

WILLY: All right. I'll go to Boston tomorrow.

HOWARD: No, no.

WILLY: I can't throw myself on my sons. I'm not a cripple!

260 HOWARD: Look, kid, I'm busy this morning.

WILLY: [*grasping HOWARD'S arm*] Howard, you've got to let me go to Boston!

HOWARD: [*hard, keeping himself under control*] I've got a line of people to see this morning. Sit down, take 265 five minutes, and pull yourself together, and then go home, will ya? I need the office, Willy. [*He starts to go, turns, remembering the recorder, starts to push off the table holding the recorder.*] Oh, yeah. Whenever you can this week, stop by 270 and drop off the samples. You'll feel better, Willy, and then come back and we'll talk. Pull yourself together, kid, there's people outside.

[*HOWARD exits, pushing the table off left. WILLY stares into space, exhausted.*]

—Arthur Miller

1. As the scene opens, Howard insistently plays with the wire recorder to

   (1) show his enthusiasm for new machines
   (2) avoid talking to Willy
   (3) explain how a wire recorder operates
   (4) introduce his family to Willy
   (5) persuade Willy to buy a wire recorder

2. "I've come to the decision that I'd rather not travel any more" (lines 94–95). What action occurs as a result of this statement? A

   (1) friendly conversation
   (2) job interview
   (3) heated argument
   (4) fair debate
   (5) fistfight

3. What is the major point of Willy's long speech (lines 148–180)?

   (1) Hundreds of salesmen and buyers attended Dave Singleman's funeral.
   (2) Willy's father was an adventurous man who lived in Alaska.
   (3) The advantages of a sales career outweigh the disadvantages.
   (4) Salesmen used to value respect and friendships as well as commissions.
   (5) Willy decided not to settle in the North.

4. How long has Willy worked for the firm? _____

5. Write two of Howard's statements that indirectly say to Willy, "You are fired."

   _____

   _____

6. From Willy's and Howard's actions, you can make judgments about their personalities and behavior. Which of the following descriptions apply to Willy? Choose three.

desperate	proud	greedy	ambitious
grateful	composed	frustrated	

7. Which of the following descriptions apply to Howard? Choose three.

impatient	appreciative	concerned	respectful
generous	insensitive	bored	

ANSWERS ARE ON PAGE 309.

WRITING ACTIVITY 3

On a separate sheet of paper, write a short scene in script form portraying a conflict between a boss and an employee. Write down the following information before you begin writing the dialogue:

- time
- characters
- place
- conflict

ANSWERS WILL VARY.

≡ GED Practice ≡

DRAMA

Read the passage below and choose the best answer to each question that follows.

Questions 1-5 refer to the following excerpt from a play.

ARE MAY AND EDDIE IN LOVE?

EDDIE: I'm not leavin'. I don't care what you think anymore. I don't care what you feel. None a' that matters. I'm not leavin'. I'm stayin' right here.
5   I don't care if a hundred "dates" walk through that door—I'll take every one of 'em on. I don't care if you hate my guts. I don't care if you can't stand the sight of me or
10   the sound of me or the smell of me. I'm never leavin'. You'll never get rid of me. You'll never escape me either. I'll track you down no matter where you go. I know exactly how
15   your mind works. I've been right every time. Every single time.

MAY: You've gotta' give this up, Eddie.

EDDIE: I'm not giving it up!

[*Pause.*]

20 MAY: [*calm*] Okay. Look. I don't understand what you've got in your head anymore. I really don't. I don't get it. *Now* you desperately need me. *Now* you can't live without me.
25   *NOW* you'll do anything for me. Why should I believe it this time?

EDDIE: Because it's true.

MAY: It was supposed to have been true every time before. Every other time.
30   Now it's true again. . . . Fifteen years I've been a yo-yo for you. I've never been split. I've never been two ways about you. I've either loved you or not loved you. And
35   now I just plain don't love you. Understand? Do you understand that? I don't love you. I don't need you. I don't want you. Do you get that? Now if you can still stay, then
40   you're either crazy or pathetic.

[*She crosses down left to table, sits in upstage chair facing audience, takes slug of tequila from bottle, slams it down on table.*]

—Sam Shepard, excerpted from *Fool for Love*, 1983

1. According to lines 1–15, what is the emotional basis for Eddie's attachment to May?

   (1) loneliness and depression
   (2) pity and guilt
   (3) obligation and commitment
   (4) love and respect
   (5) jealousy and possessiveness

2. From this excerpt, you can infer that May and Eddie's relationship is

   (1) unhealthy
   (2) caring
   (3) compassionate
   (4) unemotional
   (5) casual

3. Which of the following words best describes May's impression of Eddie's behavior?

   (1) stable
   (2) unpredictable
   (3) calm
   (4) mature
   (5) sympathetic

4. May "takes slug of tequila from bottle, slams it down on table" (lines 43–44). The playwright includes this stage direction to show May's

   (1) alcoholism
   (2) clumsiness
   (3) thirst
   (4) anger
   (5) strength

5. If May wrote a letter to Ann Landers or another advice columnist, which of the following questions would she most likely ask?

   (1) Am I too young to get married?
   (2) Will Eddie make a good husband?
   (3) Where can I find a shelter for battered women?
   (4) How can I resolve my situation with Eddie?
   (5) How long should a couple be engaged?

Questions 6–11 refer to the following excerpt from a play.

WHY IS MARGARET ANGRY?

[*At the rise of the curtain someone is taking a shower in the bathroom, the door of which is half open. A pretty young woman, with anxious lines in her face, enters the bedroom and crosses to the bathroom door.*]

MARGARET: [*shouting above roar of water*] One of those no-neck monsters hit me with a hot buttered biscuit so I have t'change!

[*MARGARET'S voice is both rapid and drawling. In her long speeches she has the vocal tricks of a priest delivering a liturgical chant, the lines are almost sung, always continuing a little beyond her breath so she has to gasp for another. Sometimes she intersperses the lines with a little wordless singing, such as "Da-da-daaaa!"*]

[*Water turns off and BRICK calls out to her, but is still unseen. A tone of politely feigned interest, masking indifference, or worse, is characteristic of his speech with MARGARET.*]

BRICK: Wha'd you say, Maggie? Water was on s' loud I couldn't hear ya. . . .

MARGARET: Well, I!—just remarked that!—one of th' no-neck monsters messed up m' lovely lace dress so I got t'—cha-a-ange. . . .

[*She opens and kicks shut drawers of the dresser.*]

BRICK: Why d'ya call Gooper's kiddies no-neck monsters?

MARGARET: Because they've got no necks! Isn't that a good enough reason?

BRICK: Don't they have any necks?

MARGARET: None visible. Their fat little heads are set on their fat little bodies without a bit of connection.

BRICK: That's too bad.

MARGARET: Yes, it's too bad because you can't wring their necks if they've got no necks to wring! Isn't that right, honey?

[*She steps out of her dress, stands in a slip of ivory satin and lace.*]

Yep, they're no-neck monsters, all no-neck people are monsters . . .

[*Children shriek downstairs.*]

Hear them? Hear them screaming? I don't know where their voice-boxes are located since they don't have necks. I tell you I got so nervous at that table tonight I thought I would throw back my head and utter a scream you could hear across the Arkansas border an' parts of Louisiana an' Tennessee. I said to your charming sister-in-law, Mae, honey, couldn't you feed those precious little things at a separate table with an oilcloth cover? They make such a mess an' the lace cloth looks *so* pretty! She made enormous eyes at me and said, "Ohhh, noooooo! On Big Daddy's birthday? Why, he would never forgive me!"

—Tennessee Williams, excerpted from *Cat on a Hot Tin Roof*, 1954

6. Which of the following words best describes Brick's attitude toward Margaret's remarks?

   (1) interested
   (2) indifferent
   (3) critical
   (4) excited
   (5) impolite

7. You can infer that this scene takes place

   (1) in the South
   (2) in the Midwest
   (3) on the West Coast
   (4) in New England
   (5) in the Southwest

8. Gooper is Brick's

   (1) father
   (2) nephew
   (3) uncle
   (4) brother-in-law
   (5) brother

9. For what special occasion is the family gathered?

   (1) the Fourth of July
   (2) Margaret and Brick's wedding anniversary
   (3) Christmas Eve
   (4) Big Daddy's birthday
   (5) Mae's graduation

10. What is the main topic of Margaret's conversation?

    (1) the children's appearance and behavior
    (2) her fondness for Big Daddy
    (3) the birthday celebration
    (4) her low opinion of her sister-in-law
    (5) the description of her dress

11. If this scene were adapted to a movie, the camera would focus on

    (1) Brick
    (2) the children
    (3) Big Daddy
    (4) Margaret
    (5) Mae

Questions 12–17 refer to the following excerpt from a play.

WHAT DO YOU LEARN ABOUT BIG WALTER?

RUTH: [*Studying her mother-in-law furtively and concentrating on her ironing, anxious to encourage without seeming to*] Well, Lord knows, we've put enough rent into this here rat trap to pay for four houses by now . . .

MAMA: [*Looking up at the words "rat trap" and then looking around and leaning back and sighing—in a suddenly reflective mood—*] "Rat trap"—yes, that's all it is. [*Smiling*] I remember just as well the day me and Big Walter moved in here. Hadn't been married but two weeks and wasn't planning on living here no more than a year. [*She shakes her head at the dissolved dream*] We was going to set away, little by little, don't you know, and buy a little place out in Morgan Park. We had even picked out the house. [*Chuckling a little*] Looks right dumpy today. But Lord, child, you should know all the dreams I had 'bout buying that house and fixing it up and making me a little garden in the back— [*She waits and stops smiling*] And didn't none of it happen. [*Dropping her hands in a futile gesture*]

RUTH: [*Keeps her head down, ironing*] Yes, life can be a barrel of disappointments, sometimes.

MAMA: Honey, Big Walter would come in here some nights back then and slump down on that couch there and just look at the rug, and look at me and look at the rug and then back at me—and I'd know he was down then . . . really down. [*After a second very long and thoughtful pause; she is seeing back to times that only she can see*] And then, Lord, when I lost that baby—little Claude—I almost thought I was going to lose Big Walter too. Oh, that man grieved hisself! He was one man to love his children.

RUTH: Ain't nothin' can tear at you like losin' your baby.

MAMA: I guess that's how come that man finally worked hisself to death like he done. Like he was fighting his own war with this here world that took his baby from him.

RUTH: He sure was a fine man, all right. I always liked Mr. Younger.

MAMA: Crazy 'bout his children! God knows there was plenty wrong with Walter Younger—hard-headed, mean, kind of wild with women— plenty wrong with him. But he sure loved his children. Always wanted them to have something—be something. That's where Brother gets all these notions, I reckon. Big Walter used to say, he'd get right wet in the eyes sometimes, lean his head back with the water standing in his eyes and say, "Seem like God didn't see fit to give the black man nothing but dreams—but He did give us children to make them dreams seem worthwhile." [*She smiles*] He could talk like that, don't you know.

RUTH: Yes, he sure could. He was a good man, Mr. Younger.

MAMA: Yes, a fine man—just couldn't never catch up with his dreams, that's all.

—Lorraine Hansberry, excerpted from *A Raisin in the Sun*, 1959

12. Which of the following words best describes Mama and Ruth's attitude toward Big Walter?

    (1) frustration
    (2) respect
    (3) disappointment
    (4) resentment
    (5) guilt

13. The major cause of Big Walter's grief was his

    (1) baby's death
    (2) financial troubles
    (3) shabby surroundings
    (4) war experiences
    (5) demanding job

14. From Mama's comments about her husband, Big Walter, you can infer that she was which type of wife?

    (1) hot-tempered
    (2) pampered
    (3) selfish
    (4) insensitive
    (5) understanding

15. According to Mama, what overall goal was Big Walter unable to accomplish?

    (1) growing a garden
    (2) buying a house
    (3) fulfilling his dreams
    (4) financing his children's education
    (5) earning a high salary

16. Why does the playwright include the gesture "Keeps her head down, ironing" (line 32) before Ruth's line of dialogue? To

    (1) show that Ruth is concerned only about her housework
    (2) emphasize that Ruth, too, understands life's disappointments
    (3) hint that Ruth is afraid to look directly at Mama
    (4) reveal Ruth's hardworking personality
    (5) stress that Ruth is bored with the conversation

17. If Big Walter were still alive, which of the following statements would he most likely support?

    (1) Children are a burden to their parents.
    (2) Children should behave as maturely as adults.
    (3) Parents should ignore their children.
    (4) Children represent the hopes for the future.
    (5) Parents should spoil their children.

ANSWERS ARE ON PAGE 309.

*Film critics Gene Siskel (left) and Roger Ebert review movies on their TV show.
Each also writes commentaries about films.*

8 Commentaries on the Arts

Nearly 25 percent of the GED Literature and the Arts Test consists of questions about commentaries on the arts. This type of nonfiction prose includes reviews and essays about these topics:

TV and Film	Performing Arts	Visual Arts	Literature
• TV shows	• music	• painting	• nonfiction
• movies	• dance	• architecture	• fiction
	• theatrical performances	• sculpture	• poetry
		• photography	• drama

Authors' approaches to writing about these artistic works depend on their purpose and readers. Examine the purpose of three kinds of commentaries: reviews, critical essays, and informative essays.

REVIEWS

Reviews of movies, plays, books, and other art forms appear in newspapers and magazines. Intended for the general reading public, reviews briefly describe the content of a piece and evaluate its strengths and weaknesses. Reviewers assume that most readers are unfamiliar with their subject. Their purpose is to present their opinion and help readers decide whether they would enjoy the work being reviewed. After reading a movie review, you might ask yourself, "According to the reviewer, should I see the movie?"

CRITICAL ESSAYS

Critical essays present a more in-depth analysis of the arts than reviews do. Critical essays are usually directed to readers who already have a solid base of knowledge about the particular art form. The author of critical essays often interprets artistic techniques, such as style and structure. The critic may also explain the meaning of a work of art and judge its merits. For example, a critical essay about the jazz singer Billie Holiday might analyze how her voice incorporated the technical and emotional qualities of Louis Armstrong's trumpet playing. (Note: The commentary selections on the GED Literature and the Arts Test do *not* require you to know anything in advance about the art forms they cover.)

INFORMATIVE ESSAYS

In informative essays, the author's intention is to educate the readers about art and artists. He or she may provide historical background, descriptive summaries, or biographical sketches. In purely informative essays, the author withholds personal judgments, because the purpose is to instruct readers rather than to persuade them to agree with his or her opinions. For example, an informative essay about art appreciation might tell readers how to look at a painting.

To prepare you for the GED Literature and the Arts Test, this chapter will present a wide range of commentaries on the arts. You will apply the reading skills discussed throughout this book. In addition, you will focus on some of the elements that reviewers, critics, and authors use in developing their topics:

- Facts and opinions

- Descriptive language

Recognizing these elements will help you determine the author's viewpoint as well as the style and the structure of commentaries on the arts.

FACTS AND OPINIONS

In Exercise 4 of Chapter 1, you learned that the fiction writer Ralph Ellison attended Tuskegee Institute in Alabama, where he studied music and composing. Through research you could prove that this statement is true. A true statement can be proved as a *fact*.

Suppose a literary critic commented, "Ralph Ellison's musical training strongly influenced his prose style. His rhythmical sentences, his attention to the sound of words, the balanced structure of his stories—all reveal how his craft as a musician was transferred to his writing." The critic's statement is an *opinion*—a judgment about Ralph Ellison's prose style. Although the critic supports the opinion with examples, it is still an opinion, a reflection of the critic's own interpretation.

You can verify the truth of factual information. In contrast, a critic's interpretation may or may not be accurate. When you read commentaries on the arts, you need to distinguish between facts and opinions. You cannot dispute the accuracy of facts. However, you have the option to agree or disagree with an author's opinion. Recognizing the difference between facts and opinions will enhance your understanding of commentaries in the following ways:

- Your literal understanding of the passage will improve if you grasp the factual information.

- You will be able to pinpoint sentences in the passage that express the author's beliefs.

- You will be able to identify facts that are used to support the critic's opinions or main idea.

Practice your skills in distinguishing facts from opinions. The following are statements about the television series "The Twilight Zone." Write *F* if the statement is a fact or *O* if it is an opinion.

_____ **1.** Rod Serling was the series' host and narrator.

_____ **2.** In 1960 and 1961, Rod Serling won an Emmy Award for "Outstanding Writing Achievements in Drama."

_____ **3.** During the 1960s, Rod Serling was the most talented and imaginative scriptwriter in Hollywood.

_____ **4.** Art Carney starred in an episode entitled "The Night of the Meek." He played a department store Santa Claus who was fired for drinking. Later in the episode, he discovered that he actually *was* Santa Claus.

_____ **5.** Art Carney's role as a drunken department store Santa Claus projects a disturbing image to young viewers.

_____ **6.** "The Night of the Meek" is a moving, sensitive story about a man's generosity and Christmas miracles.

_____ **7.** The series was telecast on CBS from 1959 to 1965.

_____ **8.** The music introducing each episode was spooky.

Did you label statements 1, 2, 4, and 7 as facts? Did you label statements 3, 5, 6, and 8 as opinions? If so, you correctly distinguished facts from opinions.

Examine these responses more closely. The accuracy of the factual statements 1, 2, 4, and 7 can be verified by research.

As you probably noticed, the descriptive words in statements 3, 5, 6, and 8 reflect the author's opinion. Statement 3 praises Rod Serling's writing as "talented" and "imaginative." Statement 5 criticizes Art Carney's portrayal of Santa Claus as "disturbing" to young viewers. In statement 6, the words *moving* and *sensitive* describe possible emotional reactions to an episode of "The Twilight Zone." In statement 8, *spooky* describes the feeling that the music might suggest to some listeners.

EXERCISE 1

Part I

Directions: Carefully read the four short commentaries about Ntozake Shange's play *For Colored Girls Who Have Considered Suicide/When the Rainbow Is Enuf.* After each commentary, write *F* if the statement is a fact or *O* if it is an opinion.

1. *For Colored Girls Who Have Considered Suicide/When the Rainbow Is Enuf* is a "choreopoem"—a theatrical production combining music, dance, and poetry. Seven black women, each wearing a dress in one of the rainbow colors, relate their personal experiences onstage. Written by Ntozake Shange, the show was first produced in November 1975. Soon after, the show was staged on Broadway for two years. The show's continued popularity reflects Shange's insightful portrayal of black women.

   _____ **(1)** A "choreopoem" combines music, dance, and poetry.

   _____ **(2)** The show was staged on Broadway for two years.

   _____ **(3)** Shange insightfully portrays the experiences of black women.

2. "[This play is a] stirringly acted, intimate production of Ntozake Shange's Tony Award–winning drama that explores the lives of seven black women, presented by Pegasus Players."

   　　　　—Excerpted from a drama review in the *Chicago Tribune,* July 25, 1986

   _____ **(1)** The show was a Tony Award–winning drama.

   _____ **(2)** The show explores the lives of seven black women.

   _____ **(3)** The production is stirringly acted and intimate.

3. "When Ntozake Shange wrote this 'choreopoem' ten years ago, it seemed like an outspoken affirmation of black women. Today, it sounds like the seven black women in this plotless play think only about black men. The adolescent poetry is flaccid and self-indulgent, and the production, despite some high-energy performances, can't pump much strength into it."

   　　　　—Excerpted from a drama review in *Chicago* magazine, August 1986

   _____ **(1)** Despite some good performances, the play is out of date.

   _____ **(2)** Shange's poetry is adolescent.

   _____ **(3)** The production of the play is weak.

4. "*Colored Girls*, as directed by Sydney Daniels, suffers from a slow start, but as Ntozake Shange's lovely poetry gets rolling, the pace picks up. And it isn't long before the Pegasus Players cast begins to make a strong connection. The tale-telling session becomes comfortable and irresistible in this cleanly delivered and forcefully presented production."

—Excerpted from a drama review in the *Chicago Sun-Times*, July 27, 1986

_____ (1) Sydney Daniels is the director.

_____ (2) The acting is performed by the Pegasus Players cast.

_____ (3) Shange's poetry is lovely.

_____ (4) The production is cleanly delivered and forcefully presented.

Part II

Directions: Reread the preceding commentaries. Then write the number of the commentary that correctly answers each of the following questions.

_____ **1.** Which commentary expresses the most negative opinion of the production?

_____ **2.** Which commentary praises Shange's poetry?

_____ **3.** Which commentary does not judge a specific production of the show?

_____ **4.** Which commentary implies that the show is out of date?

ANSWERS ARE ON PAGE 310.

WRITING ACTIVITY 1

Watch your favorite television show and write a short commentary in which you include both factual information and your opinion. In the first paragraph, record facts about the show. Include the title of the show, the names of the leading actors and the characters they portray, and a brief summary of the plot.

In the second paragraph, state your opinion of the show. Answer the following questions: Why is the show your favorite? How would you rate the actors' performances? Would you recommend the show to a friend? Use a separate sheet of paper for your commentary.

ANSWERS WILL VARY.

3. The main purpose of the second paragraph is to

   (1) discuss the architect's creativity
   (2) describe the anatomy of a turtle
   (3) interpret the symbols of Native American culture
   (4) describe the building's physical structure
   (5) convince readers to visit the Indian center

4. Which of the following words best describes the tone of the passage?

   (1) informative
   (2) persuasive
   (3) critical
   (4) entertaining
   (5) personal

5. Which of the following buildings also strongly shows how meaningful cultural symbols influence architectural design?

   (1) churches
   (2) skyscrapers
   (3) apartment complexes
   (4) factories
   (5) department stores

Questions 6–10 refer to the following excerpt from an essay.

DO FAMILIES WATCH TOO MUCH TV?

Someday, I would like to see a television series about a family that sits around the set watching a series about a family that sits around the set.

5 It might not make the Nielsen top ten, but it isn't such a strange idea. Especially when you think about what's going on right now.

Night after night, inside the tube, warm 10 and wiggly families spend their prime time "communicating" like crazy and "solving problems" together like mad. Meanwhile, outside the tube, real families sit and wait for a commercial break just to talk to 15 each other.

About the only subject that never comes up before our glazed eyes is what the medium does to our family life. But, I suppose we already know that.

20 According to a recent Gallup Poll, television comes out as a major heavy in our family lives. On the scale of problems, TV didn't rate as bad as inflation, but it ran neck-and-neck with unemployment.

25 According to a recent Roper Poll, it even causes fights. When people were asked what husbands and wives argued about, money was the champion. But television was a strong contender.

30 Husbands and wives were far more likely to fight about television than about that old standby, sex. But, considering how much more time we spend in front of the tube, that may not be such a shock.

35 To a certain extent, we blame the programs. In the Gallup Poll, for example, people worried most about the overemphasis on sex and violence. But surely half of those fights between husbands 40 and wives must be about the more fundamental issue of turning it off.

45 Deep down below our poll-taking consciousness, we know that the worst aspect of our addiction isn't what's on TV, but how long the TV is on. We can't help but be aware of what happens when we spend more time facing the screen than facing each other.

In that same Gallup Poll, a large number 50 of us said that the way to improve family life is by sharing—sharing family needs, recreational activities and chores. But when you are watching, you aren't doing. The only experience you are sharing is a 55 vicarious one.

I am absolutely convinced that the average wife feels tuned out by the twelfth consecutive weekend sports event because she *is* being tuned out. The average kid 60 develops that distant, slack-jawed, hypnotic, hooked stare because he or she *is* hooked.

In the same way, the people who spend night after night in front of the tube should worry about it. They've become an audience 65 and not a family.

—Ellen Goodman, excerpted from "Primal Screen," *Boston Globe*, July 1980

6. According to a Gallup Poll on major family problems, TV was rated about the same as

(1) inflation
(2) money
(3) unemployment
(4) sex
(5) recreation

7. The author's purpose in this excerpt is to

(1) compare the different polls that have been taken about TV
(2) explain why people spend so many hours in front of the television set
(3) describe the major source of fights between husbands and wives
(4) show that families who watch TV a lot are not communicating with each other
(5) prove that families who watch TV together communicate well with each other

8. Which word best describes what the author means when she says the wife feels "tuned out" (lines 57–59)?

    (1) disliked
    (2) sleepy
    (3) ignored
    (4) unpopular
    (5) angry

9. Which phrase best describes the author's attitude toward family TV viewing?

    (1) humorously accepting
    (2) critical of watching violence
    (3) resentful of time away from chores
    (4) hostile toward programs showing sex
    (5) concerned about the negative effect on family communication

10. The author would probably advise a modern TV-viewing family to

    (1) give everyone an equal chance to choose the programs
    (2) watch family programs that are more realistic
    (3) view fewer weekend sports events
    (4) talk to each other during commercials
    (5) participate in outside activities together

Questions 11–16 refer to the following excerpt from a critical essay.

WHAT IS DICKINSON'S POETRY LIKE?

Emily Dickinson, born in 1830 in Amherst, Massachusetts, lived a very secluded life. She was alone most of the time; she didn't know other writers. Almost
5 no one knew she wrote poetry. She wrote her poems in the midst of doing other things. She wrote them on the backs of envelopes and on other scraps of paper. These poems were discovered, and
10 published, only after her death. These circumstances probably have something to do with the peculiar way her poetry is written, the way it's unlike anyone else's— with its odd use of capitals, dashes, and
15 strange rhymes—and with its peculiar point of view. She seems to have been, more than other poets, writing just for herself.

Her way of looking at things seems, at first, innocent, like the innocence of
20 children. But Emily Dickinson knows and feels things that children don't. Her view is not so much innocent, really, as it is gentle and resigned to the way things are. It's as if
she felt that simply watching were the only
25 thing left to do. She watches nature—trees, brooks, bees, flies, flowers, snakes, wind. She watches people. She seems even to watch herself in the same way she watches everything else—with impartial curiosity and
30 from a distance.

In Emily Dickinson's poetry, the whole universe becomes very private and domestic. It is as if all of nature, all its gentle and violent forces, were noticed and
35 wondered about with the kind of simple familiarity with which you might wonder about your neighbors. And everything that happens seems almost equally important. The arrival of winter, a storm, or the coming
40 of death gets no more space than a bird's song or a fly's buzz. This makes her poems about death seem particularly strange and chilling.

—Kenneth Koch and Kate Farrell, excerpted from
Sleeping on the Wing, 1981

11. Which of the following statements expresses an opinion about Emily Dickinson?

(1) She was born in 1830 in Amherst, Massachusetts.
(2) She wrote some poems about death.
(3) Her poems were published after she died.
(4) She punctuates her poetry with dashes.
(5) Her poems show her gentle, resigned view of the world.

12. According to the excerpt, who was probably Emily Dickinson's intended audience for her poems?

(1) other poets
(2) herself
(3) children
(4) neighbors
(5) women

13. The main purpose of the second paragraph is to discuss Emily Dickinson's

(1) childlike innocence
(2) style of observation
(3) interest in people
(4) subjects of poetry
(5) curiosity about herself

14. Which of the following is *not* reflected in Emily Dickinson's poetry?

(1) a private view of the universe
(2) a unique way of writing
(3) an impression of everyday events
(4) a morbid fear of death
(5) a familiarity with nature

15. You can infer from the passage that Emily Dickinson was

(1) sociable
(2) ambitious
(3) solitary
(4) immature
(5) awesome

16. You can conclude from the passage that Emily Dickinson did *not* write a poem entitled

(1) "Bee! I'm Expecting You!"
(2) "Because I Could Not Stop for Death"
(3) "I Heard a Fly Buzz"
(4) "A Bird Came Down the Walk"
(5) "Jukebox Love Song"

ANSWERS ARE ON PAGE 312.

Literature and the Arts Post-Test

Directions: This Literature and the Arts Post-Test will give you the opportunity to evaluate your readiness for the actual GED Literature and the Arts Test.

The Post-Test contains 45 questions. These questions are based on passages of fiction and nonfiction prose, poetry, drama, and commentaries on literature and the arts.

You should take approximately 65 minutes to complete this test. At the end of 65 minutes, stop and mark your place. Then finish the test. This will give you an idea of whether or not you can finish the real GED Test in the time allotted. Try to answer as many questions as you can. A blank will count as a wrong answer, so make a reasonable guess for questions you are not sure of.

When you are finished with the test, turn to the evaluation chart on page 281. Use the chart to evaluate whether or not you are ready to take the actual GED Test and, if not, what areas need more work.

POST-TEST ANSWER GRID

1 ① ② ③ ④ ⑤	13 ① ② ③ ④ ⑤	25 ① ② ③ ④ ⑤	37 ① ② ③ ④ ⑤
2 ① ② ③ ④ ⑤	14 ① ② ③ ④ ⑤	26 ① ② ③ ④ ⑤	38 ① ② ③ ④ ⑤
3 ① ② ③ ④ ⑤	15 ① ② ③ ④ ⑤	27 ① ② ③ ④ ⑤	39 ① ② ③ ④ ⑤
4 ① ② ③ ④ ⑤	16 ① ② ③ ④ ⑤	28 ① ② ③ ④ ⑤	40 ① ② ③ ④ ⑤
5 ① ② ③ ④ ⑤	17 ① ② ③ ④ ⑤	29 ① ② ③ ④ ⑤	41 ① ② ③ ④ ⑤
6 ① ② ③ ④ ⑤	18 ① ② ③ ④ ⑤	30 ① ② ③ ④ ⑤	42 ① ② ③ ④ ⑤
7 ① ② ③ ④ ⑤	19 ① ② ③ ④ ⑤	31 ① ② ③ ④ ⑤	43 ① ② ③ ④ ⑤
8 ① ② ③ ④ ⑤	20 ① ② ③ ④ ⑤	32 ① ② ③ ④ ⑤	44 ① ② ③ ④ ⑤
9 ① ② ③ ④ ⑤	21 ① ② ③ ④ ⑤	33 ① ② ③ ④ ⑤	45 ① ② ③ ④ ⑤
10 ① ② ③ ④ ⑤	22 ① ② ③ ④ ⑤	34 ① ② ③ ④ ⑤	
11 ① ② ③ ④ ⑤	23 ① ② ③ ④ ⑤	35 ① ② ③ ④ ⑤	
12 ① ② ③ ④ ⑤	24 ① ② ③ ④ ⑤	36 ① ② ③ ④ ⑤	

Read each passage and choose the best answer to each question that follows.

Questions 1–4 refer to the following excerpt from an essay.

WHAT DO YOU NOTICE ABOUT COMMUNITIES CALLED *BARRIOS*?

The train, its metal wheels squealing as they spin along the silvery tracks, rolls slower now. Through the gaps between the cars blinks a streetlamp, and this pulsing
5 light on a barrio streetcorner beats slower, like a weary heartbeat, until the train shudders to a halt, the light goes out, and the barrio is deep asleep.

Throughout Aztlán (the Nahuatl term
10 meaning "land to the north"), trains grumble along the edges of a sleeping people. From Lower California, through the blistering Southwest, down the Rio Grande to the muddy Gulf, the darkness and mystery of
15 dreams engulf communities fenced off by railroads, canals, and expressways. Paradoxical communities, isolated from the rest of the town by concrete columned monuments of progress, and yet stranded in
20 the past. They are surrounded by change. It eludes their reach, in their own backyards, and the people, unable and unwilling to see the future, or even touch the present, perpetuate the past.

25 Leaning from the expressway or jolting across the tracks, one enters a different physical world permeated by a different attitude. The physical dimensions are impressive. It is a large section of town
30 which extends for fifteen blocks north and south along the tracks, and then advances eastward, thinning into nothingness beyond the city limits. Within the invisible (yet sensible) walls of the barrio, are many, many
35 people living in too few houses. The homes, however, are much more numerous than on the outside.

Members of the barrio describe the entire area as their home.

—Robert Ramirez, excerpted from
"The Barrio," 1974

1. Which word best describes the barrio?

    (1) isolated
    (2) sleepy
    (3) invisible
    (4) silvery
    (5) impressive

2. The purpose of the third paragraph is to

    (1) describe the homes found in the barrio
    (2) analyze why barrios are located near cities
    (3) detail the barrio's physical appearance
    (4) compare barrios with other city neighborhoods
    (5) describe the residents living in the barrios

3. Housing conditions in the barrios are

    (1) comfortable
    (2) overcrowded
    (3) modern
    (4) unusual
    (5) inhuman

4. The characteristics of the barrio most closely resemble those of

    (1) a wealthy city neighborhood
    (2) a farming community
    (3) a prison camp
    (4) a suburban community
    (5) an American Indian reservation

Questions 5–9 refer to the following excerpt from an essay.

WHAT BUSINESS VIRTUE DO AMERICANS FIND MOST DAZZLING?

They bear little resemblance to Mercury, the Roman god with the winged sandals, but they move with heroic speed. Clad in their red, white and blue polyester uniforms, the
5 drivers for Domino's Pizza spring from their vehicles with cardboard cartons and sprint up the sidewalks of millions of U.S. homes. Customers often clock them to the second, since the 2,000-shop chain promises a
10 discount if the pie takes longer than 30 minutes to arrive. To help drive home the point, Domino's sponsored a race car that finished fifth in the Indianapolis 500, with Al Unser Jr. behind the wheel.

15 Americans may value such business virtues as courtesy, reliability, economy and all that, but in the end, what really dazzles them is speed. How else to explain such an affinity for one-hour photo developing,
20 instant replay, touch-tone phones and suntanning parlors? America's entrepreneurs have responded to that imperative with some of the world's fastest products and services, ranging from frozen food to instant
25 bank loans. Like Domino's Pizza, many U.S. corporate empires were built for people in a hurry: McDonald's, Federal Express, Polaroid and Southland Corp., the operator of 7-Eleven stores. "America values speed,"
30 observes Felipe Castro, assistant professor of psychology at the University of California, Los Angeles. "The more you hustle, the more money you can make."

The culture of quickness has inspired
35 smaller operators to accelerate their pace as well. In Los Angeles, for example, time-conscious consumers can flip through the telephone book to find Speedy Attorney Service, Fast Glass & Screens, Rapid Brake
40 Service, Instant Wedding Chapel and Swift Secretarial Service. The dry-cleaning listings of any phone directory look like a thesaurus entry for the word fast, including the omnipresent 1-Hour Martinizing shops and
45 archrivals with such names as Prompt Cleaners, Presto Cleaners and One-Hour Lusterizing.

—Stephen Koepp, excerpted from "Life in the Express Lane," *Time*, June 16, 1986

5. How are the drivers for Domino's Pizza like Mercury, the Roman god?

(1) They wear winged sandals.
(2) They move with heroic speed.
(3) They compete in car races.
(4) They wear patriotic uniforms.
(5) They're America's fastest sprinters.

6. You can conclude that a thesaurus (line 42) is most similar to a

(1) phone book
(2) dictionary
(3) consumer handbook
(4) spelling book
(5) store directory

7. What is the main idea of the passage?

(1) Dry-cleaning stores advertise prompt service.
(2) McDonald's is the most famous fast-food restaurant.
(3) Americans are time-conscious consumers.
(4) The goal of American business is customer satisfaction.
(5) Consumers clock Domino's Pizza delivery trucks.

8. The quotation from Felipe Castro (lines 32–33) is effective because it

(1) interprets why Americans value speed
(2) analyzes why professors are interested in making money
(3) defines the phrase *culture of quickness*
(4) suggests that universities support major corporations
(5) proves that Americans are greedy and impatient

9. Which of the following examples would the author *not* use to support his viewpoint?

(1) microwave ovens
(2) automatic bank-teller machines
(3) overnight mail service
(4) hand-operated meat grinders
(5) instant cake mixes

Questions 10–13 refer to the following excerpt from an essay.

WHAT IS THE ATTRACTION OF DISNEY WORLD?

The moment of truth came at 3 P.M. on our second day in The Magic Kingdom of Disney World. There, in the middle of Fantasyland, a small brown bird got up and
5   flew away.

Now I know that small brown birds do this sort of thing all the time. But not, I assure you, in Disney World.

In Disney World, they may sing, they
10   may bob their heads, kick their legs, move their beaks, blink their eyes and flap their wings. But they do not fly away. And so, I stood there for several dumbfounded seconds, looking for his wire.

15   We'd been in Disney World long enough.

For two days we'd been awed and delighted by a world in which anything was mechanically possible, but a world in which the only Real Thing was the Coke.

20   The hotel we were in was so committed to the Dutch motif that anything that wasn't nailed down was molded in the shape of a wooden shoe. There, we swam in a pool in the shape of a windmill. From this absolute
25   tulip of a spot we shuttled back and forth to The Magic Kingdom. And there, too, everything was in the shape of something else.

Each bush was a topiary version of a
30   dragon, or an elephant balancing on its trunk. Trees were carved into crocodiles. Wax was molded into Presidents. An entire zoology department was created out of the endangered species known as plastic.

35   Disney World is nothing if not homage to the Mickey Mouse that lurks in each of us, an advertisement written to the Genuine Imitation. It is a tribute to the lifelike. As opposed to, say, the live.

—Ellen Goodman, excerpted from "Plastic World," *Boston Globe*, March 1979

10. In the third paragraph, what does the author mean when she says she was "looking for his [the small brown bird's] wire"? She

  (1) thought that the real bird was a mechanical one
  (2) was going to try to make the bird fly
  (3) thought the bird was broken and wanted to fix it
  (4) thought the bird was a wired-together, shaped bush
  (5) thought the plastic bird's wing had fallen off

11. The writer saw figures of presidents molded in

  (1) glass
  (2) plastic
  (3) wax
  (4) bushes
  (5) wood

12. Which of the following words best describes the tone of this excerpt?

  (1) sarcastic
  (2) romantic
  (3) suspenseful
  (4) humorous
  (5) critical

13. Which of the following souvenirs might the author be most likely to take home from Disney World?

  (1) a Coke
  (2) a plastic dinosaur
  (3) a flowering plant
  (4) an authentic antique vase
  (5) a parakeet

Questions 14–17 refer to the following excerpt from a short story.

WHAT ACTION OCCURS AT THIS DINER?

George looked up at the clock.

"If anybody comes in you tell them the cook is off, and if they keep after it, you tell them you'll go back and cook yourself. Do
5   you get that, bright boy?"

"All right," George said. "What you going to do with us afterward?"

"That'll depend," Max said. "That's one of those things you never know at the time."

10   George looked up at the clock. It was a quarter past six. The door from the street opened. A streetcar motorman came in.

"Hello, George," he said. "Can I get supper?"

15   "Sam's gone out," George said. "He'll be back in about half an hour."

"I'd better go up the street," the motorman said. George looked at the clock. It was twenty minutes past six.

20   "That was nice, bright boy," Max said. "You're a regular little gentleman."

"He knew I'd blow his head off," Al said from the kitchen.

"No," said Max. "It ain't that. Bright boy
25   is nice. He's a nice boy. I like him."

At six fifty-five George said: "He's not coming."

Two other people had been in the lunchroom. Once George had gone out to
30   the kitchen and made a ham-and-egg sandwich "to go" that a man wanted to take with him. Inside the kitchen he saw Al, his derby hat tipped back, sitting on a stool beside the wicket with the muzzle of a
35   sawed-off shotgun resting on the ledge. Nick and the cook were back to back in the corner, a towel tied in each of their mouths. George had cooked the sandwich, wrapped it up in oiled paper, put it in a bag, brought
40   it in, and the man had paid for it and gone out.

"Bright boy can do everything," Max said. "He can cook and everything. You'd make some girl a nice wife, bright boy."

45   "Yes?" George said. "Your friend, Ole Andreson, isn't going to come."

"We'll give him ten minutes," Max said.

Max watched the mirror and the clock. The hands of the clock marked seven
50   o'clock, and then five minutes past seven.

"Come on, Al," said Max. "We better go. He's not coming."

"Better give him five minutes," Al said from the kitchen.

—Ernest Hemingway, excerpted from "The Killers," 1927

14. Which word best describes the atmosphere of the diner in this scene?

(1) formal
(2) tense
(3) casual
(4) dull
(5) friendly

15. What tone of voice does Max use when he speaks to George?

(1) sarcastic
(2) polite
(3) calm
(4) agitated
(5) sincere

16. You can conclude that Max and Al's intended victim is

(1) Nick
(2) Sam
(3) the motorman
(4) George
(5) Ole Andreson

17. The conversation in the passage would also be effective in a script for a

(1) situation comedy
(2) gangster movie
(3) soap opera
(4) science fiction movie
(5) horror movie

Questions 18–21 refer to the following excerpt from a short story.

WHAT ARE THE CHARACTERS' IMPRESSIONS OF A JOCKEY NAMED BITSY BARLOW?

The three men at the corner table were a trainer, a bookie, and a rich man. The trainer was Sylvester—a large, loosely built fellow with a flushed nose and slow blue
5 eyes. The bookie was Simmons. The rich man was the owner of a horse named Seltzer, which the jockey had ridden that afternoon. The three of them drank whiskey with soda, and a white-coated waiter had
10 just brought on the main course of the dinner.

It was Sylvester who first saw the jockey. He looked away quickly, put down his whiskey glass, and nervously mashed the tip
15 of his red nose with his thumb. "It's Bitsy Barlow," he said. "Standing over there across the room. Just watching us."

"Oh, the jockey," said the rich man. He was facing the wall and he half turned his
20 head to look behind him. "Ask him over."

"God no," Sylvester said.

"He's crazy," Simmons said. The bookie's voice was flat and without inflection. He had the face of a born gambler, carefully
25 adjusted, the expression a permanent deadlock between fear and greed.

"Well, I wouldn't call him that exactly," said Sylvester. "I've known him a long time. He was O.K. until about six months ago. But
30 if he goes on like this, I can't see him lasting another year. I just can't."

"It was what happened in Miami," said Simmons.

"What?" asked the rich man.

35 Sylvester glanced across the room at the jockey and wet the corner of his mouth with his red, fleshy tongue. "A accident. A kid got hurt on the track. Broke a leg and a hip. He was a particular pal of Bitsy's. A Irish kid.
40 Not a bad rider, either."

"That's a pity," said the rich man.

—Carson McCullers, excerpted from
"The Jockey," 1936

18. Where does the scene occur?

(1) a local tavern
(2) a racetrack
(3) a locker room
(4) Miami Beach
(5) a dining room

19. The details in the first paragraph are arranged to

(1) reveal the jockey's behavior
(2) establish a conflict in the plot
(3) introduce three different characters
(4) create an atmosphere of suspense
(5) show the drinking habits of alcoholics

20. When he first noticed the jockey, Sylvester reacted by

(1) inviting the jockey to the table
(2) looking away quickly
(3) glancing across the room
(4) ordering another round of drinks
(5) criticizing the jockey's career

21. A change came about in Bitsy Barlow's character when he

(1) drank too much whiskey and soda
(2) broke his leg and hip
(3) lost a race and went crazy
(4) saw a close friend become injured on the track
(5) lost his money in a gambling bet

Questions 22–25 refer to the following poem.

WHAT RESTRICTIONS DOES A MOTHER PLACE ON HER CHILD?

A Song in the Front Yard

I've stayed in the front yard all my life.
I want a peek at the back
Where it's rough and untended and
    hungry weed grows.
5   A girl gets sick of a rose.

   I want to go in the back yard now
And maybe down the alley,
To where the charity children play.
I want a good time today.

10 They do some wonderful things.
They have some wonderful fun.
My mother sneers, but I say it's fine
How they don't have to go in at a quarter
    to nine.

15 My mother she tells me that Johnnie Mae
Will grow up to be a bad woman.
That George'll be taken to jail soon or
    late.
(On account of last winter he sold our
20   back gate.)

   But I say it's fine. Honest I do.
And I'd like to be a bad woman too,
And wear the brave stockings of night-
    black lace.
25 And strut down the street with paint on
    my face.

—Gwendolyn Brooks, 1945

22. The poem is told from whose point of view?

   (1) George's
   (2) Johnnie Mae's
   (3) a young girl's
   (4) a mother's
   (5) a neighbor's

23. Where does the girl play? In

   (1) the backyard
   (2) the alley
   (3) the street
   (4) an empty lot
   (5) the front yard

24. The details in the poem are arranged to

   (1) classify types of city neighborhoods
   (2) contrast two types of upbringings
   (3) trace the stages of criminal behavior
   (4) explain the process of child development
   (5) analyze the social causes of juvenile
      delinquency

25. The girl's mother would most likely agree that

   (1) parents stifle their children's imagination
   (2) children should ignore their parents' rules
   (3) children should choose their own friends
   (4) children require close supervision
   (5) children should imitate other people's
      behavior

POST-TEST

Questions 26–28 refer to the following poem.

WHAT IS THIS DAUGHTER FEELING AND DESCRIBING?

I'm Just a Stranger Here, Heaven Is My Home

The first sign was your hair,
unstraightened, shortened from worry,
and it had only been a year since the
    wedding,
5 but you had grown older, Mama.
I felt your usual care
in the mustard greens, sweet potatoes
    and chicken,
yet you smelled of whiskey and prayer.
10 I showed you the pictures,
asked which ones you'd like remade
and watched you fidget, unable to see
    them.
Raising your arm, you spoke of your
15   rheumatism,
it seems like life left your arm first,
like crumbs given to front yard robins.
Age and need, those simple weeds,
were gathering around and taking you
20   away.

—Carole Clemmons, 1971

26. What best expresses the main idea of this poem?

  (1) When you become an alcoholic, you neglect yourself.
  (2) You should visit your parents more often so that you can take care of their needs.
  (3) Even when they're old, mothers care for their children.
  (4) Age and need have brought about noticeable changes in Mama.
  (5) All mothers suffer from illness, old age, and depression.

27. The tone of this poem is

  (1) ironic
  (2) pleasant
  (3) sorrowful
  (4) humorous
  (5) angry

28. What is the poet describing with the phrase "those simple weeds" (line 18)?

  (1) a garden
  (2) whiskey and prayer
  (3) mama's life
  (4) age and need
  (5) rheumatism

Questions 29–32 refer to the following excerpt from a play.

WHAT IS THE CONFLICT ABOUT?

AMANDA: You're going to listen, and no more insolence from you! I'm at the end of my patience! [*He comes back toward her.*]

5 TOM: What do you think I'm at? Aren't I supposed to have any patience to reach the end of, Mother? I know, I know. It seems unimportant to you, what I'm 10 *doing*—what I *want* to do— having a little *difference* between them! You don't think that—

AMANDA: I think you've been doing things that you're ashamed of. That's 15 why you act like this. I don't believe that you go every night to the movies. Nobody goes to the movies night after night. Nobody in their right minds goes 20 to the movies as often as you pretend to. People don't go to the movies at nearly midnight, and movies don't let out at two A.M. Come in stumbling. 25 Muttering to yourself like a maniac! You get three hours' sleep and then go to work. Oh, I can picture the way you're doing down there. Moping, doping, 30 because you're in no condition.

TOM: [*wildly*] No, I'm in no condition!

AMANDA: What right have you got to jeopardize your job? Jeopardize the security of us all? How do 35 you think we'd manage if you were—

TOM: Listen! You think I'm crazy *about* the *warehouse*? [*He bends fiercely toward her slight figure.*] 40 You think I'm in love with the Continental Shoemakers? You think I want to spend fifty-five *years* down there in that—*celotex interior*! with—*fluorescent*— *tubes*! Look! I'd rather somebody 45 picked up a crowbar and

battered out my brains—than go back mornings! I *go*! Every time you come in yelling that God 50 damn *"Rise and Shine!" "Rise and Shine!"* I say to myself "How *lucky dead* people are!" But I get up. I *go*! For sixty-five dollars a month I give up all that I dream 55 of doing and being *ever*! And you say self—*self's* all I ever think of. Why, listen, if self is what I thought of, Mother, I'd be where he is—GONE! [*Pointing to* 60 *father's picture.*] As far as the system of transportation reaches! [*He starts past her. She grabs his arm.*] Don't grab at me, Mother!

—Tennessee Williams, excerpted from *The Glass Menagerie*, 1945

29. What is the main idea of lines 14–30?

(1) Tom mutters to himself like a maniac.
(2) Tom sleeps only three hours each night.
(3) Tom mopes because he is overtired.
(4) Amanda doesn't believe that Tom goes to the movies every night.
(5) Normal people don't routinely attend midnight movies.

30. Which word best describes the emotions conveyed through Tom's language?

(1) patience
(2) anger
(3) respect
(4) humor
(5) indifference

31. You can conclude that Tom's father was

(1) suicidal
(2) lucky
(3) irresponsible
(4) idealistic
(5) hardworking

32. Who would be best suited to analyze the conflict in this passage? A

(1) shoemaker
(2) factory owner
(3) filmmaker
(4) child psychologist
(5) family counselor

Questions 33–36 refer to the following excerpt from a play.

WHY IS CHELSEA COMPLAINING TO HER MOTHER?

ETHEL: Can't you be home for five minutes without getting started on the past?

CHELSEA: This house seems to set me off.

5 ETHEL: Well, it shouldn't. It's a nice house.

CHELSEA: I act like a big person everywhere else. I do. I'm in charge in Los Angeles. I guess 10 I've never grown up on Golden Pond. Do you understand?

ETHEL: I don't think so.

CHELSEA: It doesn't matter. There's just something about coming back 15 here that makes me feel like a little fat girl.

ETHEL: Sit down and tell me about your trip.

CHELSEA: [*An outburst*] I don't want to sit 20 down. Where were you all that time? You never bailed me out.

ETHEL: I didn't know you needed bailing out.

CHELSEA: Well, I did.

25 ETHEL: Here we go again. You had a miserable childhood. Your father was overbearing, your mother ignored you. What else is new? Don't you think everyone looks 30 back on their childhood with some bitterness or regret about something? You are a big girl now, aren't you tired of it all? You have this unpleasant chip 35 on your shoulder which is very unattractive. You only come home when I beg you to, and

when you get here all you can do is be disagreeable about the 40 past. Life marches by, Chelsea, I suggest you get on with it.

[*ETHEL stands and glares at CHELSEA*]

—Ernest Thompson, excerpted from *On Golden Pond*, 1979

33. When Chelsea visits Golden Pond, she feels like

(1) a grown-up
(2) a little fat girl
(3) a houseguest
(4) a released prisoner
(5) an unwelcome stranger

34. The tone of Chelsea's dialogue is

(1) calm
(2) insensitive
(3) horrifying
(4) mature
(5) emotional

35. What is the main point of Ethel's dialogue in lines 25–41?

(1) Chelsea has an overbearing father and a neglectful mother.
(2) Chelsea avoids visiting her parents at Golden Pond.
(3) Everyone looks back at his or her childhood with some bitterness or regret.
(4) Chelsea should pay more attention to events in her past.
(5) Chelsea's unhappiness as an adult stems from her miserable childhood.

36. Ethel would probably agree that

(1) parents ruin their children's lives
(2) people shouldn't bear grudges
(3) mothers don't confront the past
(4) children are forced to grow up too quickly
(5) relationships with parents improve over time

EXERCISE 7
pages 51-52

Compare your interpretations to the ones below. They do not have to be exactly the same, but they should be close.

1. Icicles are compared with a crystal monster's vicious teeth.
   Interpretation: The icicles appear menacing. The comparison emphasizes the shape and sharpness of the icicles.
2. A person is compared with a circus tightrope walker.
   Interpretation: In the person's imagination, the tightrope shows signs of breaking. The comparison conveys a sense of panic and anxiety.
3. An eyelid is compared with a window shade.
   Interpretation: Someone playing with the cord of the window shade makes you picture a window shade snapping up and down. The comparison imaginatively shows what a twitching eye looks like.
4. The sun is compared with a club.
   Interpretation: The comparison emphasizes the intensity and strength of the sun's heat beating on the man's face.
5. Lucy is compared with a general inspecting troops.
   Interpretation: The comparison suggests both Lucy's authority and her attention to details.
6. The fog is compared to grey flannel.
   Interpretation: The color and density of the fog suggest flannel fabric.

EXERCISE 8
pages 54-55

1. **No.** According to the passage, some educational counselors in trade schools are concerned mainly with selling tactics. The counselor could be distorting the truth.
2. **No.** Some vocational schools tell applicants that their test scores are amazingly high so that they will enroll in the school.
3. **Yes.** This personnel director is a reliable source of information.
4. **No.** Felicia shouldn't judge the educational quality based solely on Sandra's opinion.
5. **No.** TV commercials are sometimes deceptive. TV commercials, like salespeople, may falsely advertise the school.
6. **Yes.** Cindy should not allow the interviewer to pressure her into signing the Enrollment Agreement.

GED PRACTICE: INFERENTIAL UNDERSTANDING
pages 56-59

1. **(5) Main Idea**
   This statement summarizes the central focus of the passage. All of the paragraphs describe the personalities and the distinctive characteristics of the men.

2. **(2) Figurative Language**
   The author uses this figurative language to give readers a sense of the boomers as wandering adventurers. He implies this comparison to reveal the character of the construction workers. The statement is not literally true.
3. **(1) Figurative Language**
   Lines 18-22 explain the meaning of the figurative name *boomers.*
4. **(3) Main Idea**
   The supporting details are related directly to this statement. The fourth paragraph presents several examples of the dangers that construction workers face.
5. **(2) Supporting Details**
   You can conclude from the details describing the construction workers' life and behavior that they would not choose to settle down to a safe life.
6. **(1) Application**
   Building railroads most closely matches the construction workers' job skills and outlook on life.
7. **(1) Supporting Details**
   Lines 16-20 state that the mother is no longer pretty and that is why she picks on Connie. Therefore, you can infer that she is jealous of Connie's looks. You can assume the mother's remarks stem from her jealousy.
8. **(3) Supporting Details**
   This statement implies Connie's conceit about her appearance. There is not enough information in the passage to support the other conclusions.
9. **(5) Supporting Details**
   The mother's constant praise and approval indicate that she favors June.
10. **(4) Figurative Language**
    Trash is considered worthless. The phrase "trashy daydreams" suggests that her mother thinks that Connie's inner thoughts are worthless.
11. **(2) Supporting Details**
    The father does not interact with his family. Since he reads the newspaper during supper, you can assume he isn't talking to his wife or daughters. You also know that he goes to bed after supper.
12. **(2) Application**
    A family counselor is trained to analyze the relationships within a family.
13. **(3) Figurative Language**
    The author uses this comparison to show how a creative idea is similar to a pregnancy. He carries within him a story that he can bring to life.
14. **(2) Main Idea**
    The paragraph describes in detail the way his father told stories.

15. **(1) Supporting Details**
    The author respects his father's talents. You can conclude from the second paragraph that his father probably inspired the author to write stories.

16. **(2) Supporting Details**
    Becoming a writer seems to be a mixed blessing. The phrase "cursed my fate" suggests the difficulties and struggles that the author experiences.

17. **(4) Application**
    Because an artist produces original work, he or she would most likely identify with the author's struggle for creative expression.

CHAPTER 3: ANALYZING STYLE AND STRUCTURE

EXERCISE 1
page 66

1. conversational	**5.** formal
2. conversational	**6.** informal
3. formal	**7.** informal
4. informal	**8.** informal

EXERCISE 2
page 67

1. formal	**4.** conversational
2. conversational	**5.** informal
3. formal	

Explanation: All examples of formal diction address a select reading audience and use difficult vocabulary. The example of informal diction addresses a general reading audience and uses simpler vocabulary. Conversational diction most closely resembles people's speech.

EXERCISE 3
page 69

1. **(4)** The second sentence states, "I built emotional bridges in the imagination to link me to the world and to other people."
2. **(1)** The central theme is that, as a child, Paz could stretch his imagination to transform time and space to connect to the past or the future.
3. **(1)** In the fifth sentence, Paz states, "The garden soon became the center of my world."

EXERCISE 4
page 72

1. **(1)** Given the frightening content of the speaker's statement, it's reasonable to infer that he would adopt a threatening tone.
2. **(3)** Statements such as "what a weird age to be male" and "well, things tend to be less than perfect" indicate that the tone is funny.

3. **(1)** A somber tone would be appropriate in describing the depressing weather and sad situation.
4. **(4)** It's likely that a speaker would sound intimidating when describing the tortures of the damned.

EXERCISE 5
pages 76-77

Numbers should be listed in the following order: 5, 3, 8, 1, 9, 2, 4, 7, 6.

EXERCISE 6
pages 80-81

1. d		**5.** e	
2. f		**6.** a	
3. b		**7.** c	
4. g			

EXERCISE 7
page 83

1. The purpose of this passage is to compare and contrast TV shows with the real world.
2. In paragraph 3, a TV cabdriver is compared and contrasted with a real cabdriver.
3. In paragraph 5, an emergency ward on TV is compared with an emergency ward in a real hospital.
4. According to Dr. Applebaum, television shows present children with an inaccurate picture of real-life situations.

EXERCISE 8
page 85

1. **(4)** In lines 11–13, Huck says, "I didn't need anybody to tell me that [killing a spider] was an awful bad sign and would fetch me some bad luck. . . ."
2. **(4)** In lines 14–15, Huck says, "I was scared and most shook the clothes off of me."

GED PRACTICE: ANALYZING STYLE AND STRUCTURE
pages 86-89

1. **(3) Tone**
   The article is meant to be funny.
2. **(5) Style**
   The author's conversational writing style would also be appropriate for a script of a TV comedy series.
3. **(1) Structure**
   The author explains a process—how to kick a machine.
4. **(2) Style**
   A conversation is the author's primary method for revealing the people's reactions to the coffee machine.

5. (3) Diction

Downsizing is the euphemism (pleasant-sounding substitute) big companies use for *layoffs* and *firings*.

6. (2) Structure

The first two paragraphs state the main idea—that word watchers have compiled a list of "misused, overused and useless" words.

7. (4) Tone

The writer's tone is informal and lighthearted. The excerpt plays with words to make fun of how they are used.

8. (4) Diction and Tone

Although the storyteller admits that he is nervous, he refuses to believe that he is, in fact, mad. The way he repeats certain phrases also conveys that he is emotionally unbalanced.

9. (1) Tone

The storyteller discusses his actions of the week before the murder. The way he sneaks around the old man's room every night causes the reader to wonder how he actually committed the crime. By leaving out this information, the storyteller builds suspense.

10. (5) Structure

In the fourth paragraph, the storyteller organizes his account in chronological order to show the sequence of his actions preceding the crime.

CHAPTER 4: NONFICTION PROSE

EXERCISE 1
pages 94-95

1. (2) In lines 22–23, Jennifer says, "With last Christmas and bills, we've gone through all the money we had. . . ." In lines 58–59, community services representative Chris Marston says, "It's amazing how people will spend everything on Christmas presents. . . ."

2. (5) The last paragraph states that 80 percent of jobs are not found through newspaper ads but through the "hidden job market"—by word of mouth.

3. (4) Lines 70–71 explain that *hidden job market* refers to unadvertised jobs.

4. (1) In lines 41–43, Dr. Cahill says, "He [an unemployed man] needs to find . . . a way to connect with the community."

EXERCISE 2
page 96

1. (5) The passage details the demanding work of a homemaker. As the homemaker says, "There are mothers that work eleven, twelve hours a day. . . . When do you get a break, really? You don't."

2. (1) In lines 18–19, the homemaker mentions washing clothes.

3. (2) She states, "Welfare makes you feel like you're nothing. Like you're laying back and not doing anything and it's falling in your lap" (lines 13–15).

EXERCISE 3
page 97

1. MBWA means that managers care enough about what's going on in the organization to walk around and find out from the employees. **TQM** has as its goal instilling pride in getting the best possible job done for the organization.

2. The best techniques for solving employee problems must come from a genuine caring attitude.

EXERCISE 4
page 98

1. (4) When addressing high school audiences, the author's major message is "You will need that diploma" (line 7).

2. (1) invalid—The author believes that too many athletes are uneducated. However, he does not suggest that they are stupid but that they have the potential to learn.

(2) valid—In the third paragraph, the author summarizes the realities of professional sports. He implies that athletes seldom foresee these problems.

(3) valid—In the second paragraph, the author implies that high school athletes spend more time on the athletic field than in the library.

(4) invalid—Although the author states that there are some stars "earning millions," he doesn't suggest that they are overpaid.

(5) invalid—You can conclude that some athletes spend sleepless nights worrying about their future. They are not staying awake to study.

EXERCISE 5
page 99

1. (4) Throughout the excerpt, the writer gives examples of fans and scouts who know everything about Felipe that relates to basketball because they believe he'll be a big star someday.

2. (2) "The white men"—meaning scouts and fans—are everywhere, following Felipe and keeping close track of his basketball career.

3. (1) Generally, people like to follow someone who they think is going to be a winner. They're hanging around Felipe because they expect that he will someday be a star player.

EXERCISE 6
pages 100-101

1. **(4)** From paragraph 4 to the end, the writer describes psychological and social benefits of playing video games.
2. **(1)** In several instances, the writer suggests that playing video games will help children become well adjusted. For example, in lines 49-51, he states, "For some youngsters, video game prowess represents a way of gaining acceptance within their peer groups."
3. **(1)** The excerpt is directed primarily at parents of adolescents. The author tries to persuade parents that playing video games will help their children's self-confidence and will help parents and their youngsters get along better.
4. **(5)** The concluding paragraph states that video games can open "new avenues of communication and discussion."
5. **(3)** In the second paragraph, the writer quotes a psychologist.

EXERCISE 7
pages 102-103

1. **(1)** relaxation
   (2) release from daily stress
   (3) cure for loneliness
2. **(2)** Dr. Haun states in line 24 that watching soap operas makes college students feel "less homesick."
3. **(5)** The author cites nothing but benefits from watching soap operas. Therefore, you can infer that she would agree that watching soap operas is therapeutic.
4. **(1)** **F**—Dr. Haun states that "there doesn't seem to be any relationship between socio-economic levels, occupations, or education among those who watch soaps" (lines 34-35).
   (2) **F**—Dr. Cassata states that "the characters have become so complex, it's hard to tell the good guy from the bad guy" (lines 40-41).
   (3) **T**—Dr. Cassata states, "It gives the person another way of thinking about the problem" (line 7).
   (4) **F**—According to Dr. Haun's research, the number of male viewers is steadily climbing.
5. **(2)** Using the research and observations of professors Haun and Cassata—experts in the field—strengthens the author's own viewpoint.

EXERCISE 8
pages 104-105

1. **(2)** Line 1 says that he is a Detroit area teacher.
2. **(3)** The story is told to make the point that children have been taught to be unreasonably afraid of adult strangers.

3. **(5)** Lines 13-14 suggest that only paper cartons "bear the pictures of missing children."
4. **(2)** The author draws this conclusion in the last sentence of the passage.

EXERCISE 9
pages 106-107

1. **(5)** Although the writer does mention each of the other options, his overall message is one of simple, everyday consideration for people with disabilities.
2. **(1)** The writer expects to be treated as a mature, intelligent adult.
3. **(3)** The writer points out with irony that even a person who specializes in proper behavior may be insensitive when it comes to dealing with a disabled person.
4. **(3)** In lines 95-96, the author says, "The unifying theme of all the suggestions above is inclusiveness."
5. **(2)** In lines 45-48, the author says, "Those of us who can't stand get tired of talking to belt buckles. Try to park us near chairs . . . so people speaking with us can be at our level."

EXERCISE 10
pages 108-109

1. **(2)** Melvin H. Purvis, head of the Chicago office, organized his men to trap Dillinger. Therefore, you can conclude that the shooting occurred in Chicago.
2. **(5)** Line 19 states that *Manhattan Melodrama* was a "feature film."
3. **(3)** The action-packed description resembles the writing style of gangster novels.
4. Numbers should be listed in the following order: 3, 4, 2, 6, 5, 1.

EXERCISE 11
page 110

1. Kiowas
2. **Sight:** "tortoises crawl about on the red earth"
   "great green and yellow grasshoppers are everywhere in the tall grass"
   "green belts along the rivers and the creeks"
   Hearing: "grass . . . cracks beneath your feet"
   Touch: "grasshoppers . . . sting the flesh"
   "grass turns brittle"
3. **(1)** The author uses figurative language to emphasize the intense summer heat. The plants are not literally on fire.
4. **(4)** The author vividly describes colors and the scenery. He uses words to paint a picture of the landscape.
5. **(1)** "Rises out of the plain" is the context clue that supports the answer that a knoll is a hill.

GED PRACTICE: NONFICTION PROSE
pages 111-115

1. (2) Main Idea and Structure
The entire passage explains the procedure that Mr. Hagenlocher follows in sketching a suspect.

2. (4) Supporting Details
Lines 1-2 state that "Mr. Hagenlocher tries to put witnesses at ease."

3. (2) Supporting Details
Lines 15-16 state, "Witnesses are asked to leaf through these [mug shots] to try to find a similar face."

4. (4) Supporting Details
According to the passage, Mr. Hagenlocher poses all of the other questions except this one.

5. (5) Style and Structure
Quotations from Mr. Hagenlocher explain the process of sketching suspects from his viewpoint.

6. (3) Application
A portrait painter is also skilled in drawing people's faces.

7. (2) Main Idea
The main idea is stated in the most well-known sentence from this speech: "Ask not what your country can do for you—ask what you can do for your country."

8. (4) Supporting Details
In lines 4-6, Kennedy states that "each generation of Americans has been summoned to give testimony to its national loyalty."

9. (3) Style and Structure
Kennedy's speech is intended to be an inspirational message to the American people. For example, by appealing to the power of energy, faith, and devotion, he attempts to foster the highest ideals. The speech encourages Americans to involve themselves in achieving the country's goals.

10. (2) Supporting Details
In lines 25-26, Kennedy states, "I do not shrink from this responsibility—I welcome it."

11. (3) Style and Application
The concluding sentence contains religious language such as *blessing* and *God's work*.

12. (5) Supporting Details
Classes were taught "by instructors who came from such places as Harvard and Boston universities" (lines 3-5).

13. (1) Supporting Details
The last sentence of the first paragraph indicates that the debates were popular with both the inmate debaters and their audience. The passage also says that well-read inmates among the popular debaters were "almost celebrities" (line 33).

14. (4) Supporting Details
Lines 27-29 state that "an inmate was smiled upon if he demonstrated an unusually intense interest in books." Therefore, you can infer that the prison officials approved of this activity.

15. (3) Figurative Language
Malcolm X is using this expression figuratively, not literally. He is describing the "well-read inmates."

16. (3) Supporting Details
Lines 45-47 state, "It always seemed to catch me right in the middle of something engrossing." In other words, the "lights out" rule interrupted Malcolm X's reading.

17. (2) Main Idea
Throughout the passage, Malcolm X conveys his enthusiasm for "being able to read and *understand*." He also admires the other inmates who show a desire to learn.

18. (3) Application
Malcolm X and some of his fellow inmates are examples of individuals who took the initiative to educate themselves. Therefore, you can conclude that if Malcolm X were alive today, he would believe strongly in self-education.

CHAPTER 5: PROSE FICTION

EXERCISE 1
page 122

1. (2) The children keep hearing the phrase "There must be more money!"
2. (5) The children are playing in their nursery.
3. (3) The emphasis on money has filled the house with tension.

EXERCISE 2
page 123

1. (3) References such as "the punishment block (the stone prison inside the camp))," "barbed-wire fence," and "prisoners" support the idea that this is a prison camp.
2. (5) The details describing the environment of the prison camp and the extremely cold weather create an atmosphere of oppression.
3. Phrases referring to the weather include
freezing cold
boots crunching on the snow
the thermometer hung, caked over with ice
freezing weather
frost-covered rail
they all felt cold

EXERCISE 3
page 127

1. (5) Lines 3–5 state, "it symbolized all the misery of the plural South African society."
2. (3) Karlie defies the laws of South African society.
3. (2) Karlie shows courage when he defies South Africa's system of racial discrimination.
4. (5) Karlie's actions suggest that he would also support the human rights movement in the United States.

EXERCISE 4
page 133

Part I
1. Tony grew up in a crowded, poverty-stricken neighborhood.
2. sixteen
3. juvenile delinquents
4. He was in a car with boys who robbed a liquor store.
5. Tony would marry Rosa and manage a candy store for her father.

Part II
6. Tony's life was troubled and unfocused.
7. By marrying Rosa, Tony gained a business.

EXERCISE 5
page 135

1. riding clothes
2. **Age:** thirty
   Hair color: "straw-haired" or blond
3. "hard mouth"; "arrogant eyes"; "cruel body"
4. Words or phrases suggesting Tom's strength and force include
   sturdy
   dominance
   leaning aggressively forward
   enormous power
   great pack of muscle
   body capable of enormous leverage
5. **(2)** From the descriptive words in the passage, you can infer that Nick's attitude toward Tom is critical.

EXERCISE 6
page 136

1. Pepi
2. one of the men from Detroit
3. Joe Sansone
4. Pepi
5. one of the men from Detroit

EXERCISE 7
pages 138-139

1. (3) The general topic that the brothers are discussing is Sonny's choice of careers.
2. (1) Sonny's brother says in lines 27–28, "I was furious."
3. (4) You can conclude from these lines of dialogue that Sonny sincerely wants to become a jazz musician.
4. (1) V   (5) I
   (2) V   (6) I
   (3) I   (7) V
   (4) I   (8) V

EXERCISE 8
pages 140-141

Part I
Numbers should be listed in the following order: 3, 4, 7, 2, 6, 1, 5

Part II
1. F   5. F
2. F   6. F
3. T   7. T
4. T   8. T

EXERCISE 9
pages 144-145

Your interpretations may differ.
1. Hogs are compared to huge spotted stones.
   Interpretation: The comparison emphasizes the coloring of the hogs.
2. A man is compared to a crow.
   Interpretation: The man makes birdlike movements.
3. A woman's eyes are compared to two chips of green bottle glass.
   Interpretation: The woman has sparkling green eyes.
4. Mrs. Watts's grin is compared to the blade of a sickle.
   Interpretation: The comparison exaggerates the shape of her smile.
5. Hair is compared to dripping gravy.
   Interpretation: The comparison describes the look of a woman's hair. The thin hair looks like ham gravy trickling down a surface.

EXERCISE 10
page 146

1. (4) Painted savages suggest an image of wildness.
2. (1) Serpents are usually characterized as being evil creatures. The coiled chimney smoke seems wicked.

3. (3) The comparison suggests that the steam engine functions like a crazed animal.

4. (2) The descriptions of the buildings, the chimney smoke, the river, and the steam engines reveal the ugliness of this industrial city.

5. (5) The descriptions of the buildings, river, and steam engine appeal to the sense of sight. The dye dumped in the river is described as "ill-smelling" (line 11). The windows are described as "rattling" (line 13).

EXERCISE 11
pages 150-151

1. (5) Paragraph 2 says that his name is on the list of those killed in a "railroad disaster."

2. (1) The second sentence states that "it was her sister Josephine who told her."

3. (3) The story focuses on the woman's thoughts and feelings as she sits alone in her room directly after learning that her husband has died.

4. (3) The theme is summed up in the closing lines: "But she saw beyond that bitter moment [when she saw her husband in his casket] a long procession of years to come that would belong to her absolutely. And she opened and spread her arms out to them in welcome."

5. (4) The description of new life and hope in paragraphs 5 and 6 foreshadows, or hints at, the woman's feelings about life without her husband.

6. (2) Since the story is about a wife's struggle for personal freedom, it is likely that the author would agree that women should lead their own lives.

EXERCISE 12
pages 152-157

1. Waterbury
2. 2, 5, 1, 3, 4
3. Character: Famous doctor
Situation: Performing surgery on a millionaire banker
Character: Accused murderer
Situation: Testifying on the witness stand
Character: Captain during the war
Situation: Volunteering to fly alone in a bomber plane
4. The following lines of dialogue reveal Mrs. Mitty's bossiness and critical attitude toward her husband:
"Not so fast! You're driving too fast! What are you driving so fast for?" (lines 14-15)
"Remember to get those overshoes while I'm having my hair done." (lines 26-27)
"You're not a young man any longer." (line 29)
"Why don't you wear your gloves? Have you lost your gloves?" (lines 30-31)
"Couldn't you have put them on in the store?" (lines 151-152)
"I'm going to take your temperature when I get you home." (lines 153-154)

5. (4) The commander, the doctor, the accused murderer, the captain, and the man before the firing squad are heroic characters. They all demonstrate strength and courage.

6. (5) The events of the story reveal this theme. Walter Mitty's daydreams add excitement to his life.

7. (2) Walter Mitty is portrayed as a comic character. The tone of the story is humorous.

GED PRACTICE: PROSE FICTION
pages 158-161

1. (5) Supporting Detail
The fact that an arrested person was treated violently is supported by the description that away from the crowd, the police "whaled him with their clubs" (line 21).

2. (2) Structure and Point of View
The second and third paragraphs describe the scene from Tod's point of view.

3. (4) Characterization
Lines 25-26 state that Tod "began to get frightened."

4. (4) Figurative Language
The author makes a comparison between a reporter and a revivalist preacher speaking in a "rapid, hysterical voice" to create an image of someone speaking in an agitated manner.

5. (2) Point of View
References such as "They had enough to do without chasing him" and "he began to get frightened" indicate that the story is being told by a narrator acting as an outside, all-knowing reporter. Not involved in the action himself, the narrator relates the events and the thoughts and feelings of the characters.

6. (2) Theme
The author reveals this theme by describing the crowd's behavior as if it were one personality. The crowd is portrayed as a mob out of control. As a result, individual personalities do not seem to exist.

7. (2) Application
Newspapers frequently report similar mob scenes at rock concerts.

8. (3) Setting
Miss Havisham is surrounded by clothing and jewelry. Since she appears to be in the middle of dressing, you can infer that the scene takes place in her bedroom.

9. (3) Characterization
You learn about Miss Havisham's character from her physical appearance and the condition of her surroundings.

10. (1) Characterization
Clues supporting the inference that she is wealthy include rich materials and the sparkling jewels around Miss Havisham's neck and on the table.

11. (1) Setting

The phrases *faded and yellow* and *withered like the dress* suggest decay.

12. (5) Point of View

In answer to the question *Who is it?* the response *Pip, ma'am* and the use of the pronoun *I* indicate that the narrator is the character Pip. He describes Miss Havisham and the setting from his point of view.

13. (1) Figurative Language

The purpose of this comparison is to show how the author presents the action-filled plot.

14. (3) Point of View

Lines 18–22 support the response that the author tells the novel from Bigger's point of view.

15. (3) Style and Structure

References such as "building of a well-constructed book," "I told of Bigger's life in close-up, slow-motion," and "I restricted the novel" imply that the author deliberately constructed the novel to achieve a certain effect.

16. (2) Figurative Language

The author uses the comparison to illustrate how he wants the reader to experience the story. The reader should feel that he is a special audience watching Bigger's drama unfold.

17. (3) Main Idea

The focus of this passage is to show the techniques of writing a novel. The author discusses methods of presenting plot, characterization, and point of view.

18. (3) Application

It is a journalist's job to report on factual events.

CHAPTER 6: POETRY

EXERCISE 1
pages 166-167

1. **Lines 2 and 4:** play, today
   Lines 6 and 8: wild, child
   Lines 10 and 12: me, free
   Lines 14 and 16: fire, choir
   Lines 18 and 20: sweet, feet
   Lines 22 and 24: place, face
   Lines 26 and 28: wild, child
   Lines 30 and 32: shoe, you
2. **(1)** "For the dogs are fierce and wild, / And clubs and hoses, guns and jail / Aren't good for a little child." (lines 6–8)
   "For I fear those guns will fire." (line 14)
   (2) "Her eyes grew wet and wild." (line 26)
   (3) "She clawed through bits of glass and brick" (line 29)
   (4) "O here's the shoe my baby wore, / But, baby, where are you?" (lines 31–32)

3. **(1)** F
   (2) T
   (3) T
   (4) T

EXERCISE 2
pages 170-171

1. **(3)** The title of the poem ("Tribal Cemetery"), the description of the tombstone (first stanza), and line 13 support this response.
2. **(2)** The pronoun *I* refers to the father's daughter—the speaker of the poem.
3. **(2)** The repetition of *English words* emphasizes that English was an alien language for the father, a Native American, to learn.
4. **(1)** The daughter's tone of respect for her father and his culture reveals her pride.
5. **(1)** **I**—The father was a veteran in World War I. However, no additional details are given to suggest that he was awarded medals for bravery.
   (2) **V**—The father went to the Mission School when he was twelve. He was apparently forced to learn white America's social customs and language. You can conclude that this education gradually removed him from his original heritage.
   (3) **I**—The father learned "to pray to the Catholic God" (line 26) when he attended the Mission School. Therefore, he did not practice only his native religion during his life.
   (4) **V**—In the concluding lines of the poem, the speaker states that she and her children know only English words. Because they don't understand her father's language, you can infer that they are disconnected from an important part of their Native American roots.
   (5) **V**—You can assume that before the father attended the Mission School, he was probably accustomed to going barefoot, eating without silverware, practicing his tribe's religion, and speaking his tribe's language. The training at the Mission School was evidently designed to make him conform to white American culture and "white ways of thinking."
   (6) **V**—Because of their different language and culture, non-English-speaking immigrants are often alienated from mainstream American society. They, too, are pressured to adopt a new cultural identity.

EXERCISE 3
page 175

1. The number 5 on the fire engine. The title of the poem, "The Great Figure," provides you with an important clue.
2. in a rainy, dark city
3. **(2)** The words *moving/tense* immediately follow the word *firetruck*.
4. "gong clangs," "siren howls," "wheels rumbling"

EXERCISE 4

pages 179-183

1. **(2)** The title of the poem, "I Wandered Lonely as a Cloud," supports this response.
2. **(1)** Lines 7-9 compare the arrangement of daffodils with the stars in the Milky Way, the galaxy in which our solar system is located.
3. **(5)** The poet compares the motion of the flowers to the motion of dancers.
4. **(3)** Watching the flowers changes the speaker's mood from sad to happy.

EXERCISE 5

pages 184-185

1. two sisters, a father, a mother, and a stepmother
2. The speaker compares her mother's figure to a rag bag.
3. The speaker compares her mother's figure to a mattress.
4. A wedding ring. You know from lines 11-12 that he did not wear a wedding ring during his marriage to the speaker's mother. In addition, you know that her father left her mother to marry the second wife (lines 16-17). These clues, along with the legend on the photo (lines 13-15), imply that his second marriage meant more to him than his first.
5. Your summary should include the following information: Two sisters are looking at an old photograph of their father. The mother, a woman who is apparently showing her age, is also present. One of the sisters mistakenly assumes that the photo was originally given to her mother. The sister then realizes that the photo belonged to her father's second wife. The father divorced her mother to marry this woman.

EXERCISE 6

page 186

1. The woman is in the living room.
2. Scattered around are record albums.
3. He emphasizes how much he is intrigued by the dimples on the woman's cheeks, arms, and legs. The repetition also produces a musical effect.
4. The woman "loves" Johnny Mathis's music and his looks.
5. **(4)** *Dances* and *whirls* emphasize the rhythmic quality of Mathis's voice. *Windblown snow* suggests softness. The entire description uses figurative language to show the beauty of Mathis's voice.

EXERCISE 7

page 187

1. 8:00 A.M., lunchtime
2. "*splintery* redwood rafters"; "*Itch* of haydust in the / *sweaty* shirt and shoes"

3. "Grasshoppers *crackling* in the weeds"
4. seventeen, sixty-eight
5. He said that he would hate to buck hay all his life.

GED PRACTICE: POETRY

pages 189-193

1. **(5) Supporting Details**
   Lines 13-14 support this response: "He never learned a trade; he just sells gas, / Checks oil, and changes flats."
2. **(2) Figurative Language**
   The poet is using personification to show the physical appearance of the gas pumps. He implies that they resemble human beings. Specifically, the hoses seem to be "rubber elbows."
3. **(4) Main Idea**
   The descriptive details relate to Flick's outstanding athletic performance.
4. **(5) Figurative Language**
   This simile reveals Flick's skill in handling the basketball.
5. **(2) Drawing Conclusions**
   From descriptions of Flick's actions at the gas station, you can conclude that he misses playing basketball— "As a gag, he dribbles an inner tube." When the speaker says, "But most of us remember anyway," he is referring to Flick's exciting moments on the basketball court. In contrast, his work at the gas station is dull and unmemorable.
6. **(3) Understanding Words in Context**
   The "bright applauding tiers" in line 23 refer to the racks used by restaurants to display candies for sale. Therefore, you can conclude that Necco Wafers, Nibs, and Juju Beads are sweets.
7. **(1) Main Idea**
   By comparing and contrasting moments from Flick's past with his present situation, the poem makes a statement about the short-lived fame of high school athletes. The title of the poem, "Ex-Basketball Player," also emphasizes that Flick's sports career is over.
8. **(2) Application**
   The poem discusses what happened to a star high school athlete after he graduated. An article about this topic would most likely appear in a sports magazine.
9. **(2) Characterization**
   These references imply that the speakers are poor and hardworking: "So on we worked, and waited for the light, / And went without the meat, and cursed the bread."
10. **(3) Figurative Language**
    These words are associated with a person who holds a regal position.

11. **(5) Supporting Details**
    Richard Cory "put a bullet through his head." In other words, he kills himself.
12. **(3) Making Inferences**
    Most people who commit suicide suffer from serious personal problems. These problems are not apparent to the townspeople.
13. **(1) Figurative Language**
    The word *light* is used figuratively, not literally. The poor townspeople are referring to their desire for brighter, happier days.
14. **(4) Application**
    This answer restates the central message of the poem as the title of a magazine article. Richard Cory's wealth does not protect him from the circumstances that lead to his suicide.
15. **(2) Figurative Language**
    The title of the poem, "Daybreak," is an important clue. The first stanza uses figurative language to describe the dawn—the time when "the light starts up / In the east."
16. **(1) Style and Structure**
    The break in stanzas is similar to a paragraph break signaling a change in topic.
17. **(5) Making Inferences**
    The speaker indirectly explains how picking onions causes painful blisters on the farm workers' hands.
18. **(3) Figurative Language**
    The onions lie asleep or motionless underground. The word *unplug* is an imaginative way of saying *uproot*.
19. **(1) Figurative Language**
    The speaker is showing the force of the raindrops striking the ground. The impact seems to break the raindrops like the broken fingers of a hand.
20. **(4) Main Idea**
    The poem details the grueling physical work of onion pickers.
21. **(2) Application**
    When consumers purchase a factory-made product, they probably don't appreciate the hours of hard labor required to manufacture the product. Similarly, the poem suggests that people who buy onions never think of the onion pickers working in the fields.

CHAPTER 7: DRAMA

EXERCISE 1
page 199

1. **(1)** [*Almost in tears.*] (line 25)
   (2) [*Stands up and throws the mouse as far as he can. . .*] (line 31)
   (3) [*. . .GEORGE puts his hand on LENNIE'S shoulder for a moment.*] (lines 39–40)
2. **(1)** "Blubbering like a baby. Jesus Christ, a big guy like you!" (lines 36–37)
   (2) "What, George? I ain't got no mouse." (lines 16–17)
   (3) "Don't you think I could see your feet was wet where you went in the water to get it?" (lines 34–35)
3. **(1) I**—When Lennie starts crying, George tries to console him. George says that Lennie can get another mouse.
   (2) I—Both George and Lennie use conversational language and ungrammatical expressions like *ain't.*
   (3) V—You can infer that George controls the relationship. He tells Lennie what to do and how to behave.
   (4) V—Although Lennie is a grown man, he thinks and acts like a child. He cries when George scolds him. Lennie depends on George because Lennie's judgment is evidently inferior.

EXERCISE 2
page 205

1. **(4)** Oscar states in lines 5–7 that the two men live in "a big eight-room apartment."
2. **(3)** All the stage directions referring to Felix describe his physical movements and housecleaning.
3. **(2)** *Angrily* is in *italicized print* in line 39.
4. **(1)** Felix clears the dishes, glasses, and coasters from the table. He also empties and wipes the ashtrays.
5. **(2)** The dialogue between Felix and Oscar clearly reveals their different housekeeping habits. Oscar is annoyed because Felix is always cleaning the apartment.

EXERCISE 3
pages 207-208

1. **(3)** From the tone of the conversation, we can infer that the characters are having a friendly argument.
2. **(4)** In lines 38–40, Troy says, "I'll do my shopping where the people been good to me."
3. **(2)** Several details suggest that Rose is practical. She's thrifty, she has no illusions about her son's making a career of football, and she's willing to go along with the changing times.

4. (5) Troy argues that his son foolishly believes he's going to make a living playing football because he was recruited by a college team. Rose, on the other hand, thinks it's an honor and "just something the boys in school do."

5. (1) Bono tells about living in poverty for six years before he and Lucille could better themselves. Then Rose talks about grocery shopping where she can save money. Afterward, Troy comments that he is grateful his sons are working—"things getting tight around here"—and that Cory should learn how to fix cars so he can earn a living. Finally, Troy uses figurative language to describe his lack of money.

EXERCISE 4
pages 210-212

1. at a table

2. (5) Nora does not mean this statement literally. She is using a financial expression as a figure of speech. She wants to end the marriage.

3. (3) Nora is using a figure of speech to describe her roles as wife and daughter. Helmer and her father have both treated Nora like a doll—a plaything, not a person.

4. Nora plays a make-believe role in an unreal home. (Your answer may differ slightly.)

5. (1) F—Nora says, "I'm saying that we've never sat down seriously together and tried to get to the bottom of anything" (lines 21–23).

   (2) T—Helmer does not criticize the marriage and resents Nora's description of their relationship. He asks in line 39, "How can you speak of our marriage like that?"

   (3) T—Although Helmer declares his love for Nora, she replies, "You never loved me. You've thought it fun to be in love with me, that's all" (lines 30–31).

   (4) F—Helmer asks, "You mean I should constantly go and involve you in problems you couldn't possibly help me with?" (lines 19–20). This question implies that Helmer considers himself superior to Nora.

   (5) F—Nora tells Helmer, ". . . you've never understood me" (line 25).

   (6) T—Nora tells Helmer, "And you've always been so kind to me" (lines 53–54).

6. Answers will vary.

EXERCISE 5
pages 214-221

1. (2) As the scene opens, Willy says, "Like to have a little talk with you, Howard" (line 9). By playing with the wire recorder, Howard avoids the conversation with Willy.

2. (3) Willy's decision not to travel causes a heated argument between Willy and Howard. Their argument is the central action depicted in this scene.

3. (4) These lines from Willy's speech summarize the main point—the meaning of a sales career when Willy was a young man: "There was respect, and comradeship, and gratitude in it. Today it's all cut and dried . . ." (lines 176–178).

4. thirty-four years

5. "I don't want you to represent us" (line 239). "I think you need a good long rest, Willy" (line 242).

6. Three descriptions that apply to Willy are *proud*, *desperate*, and *frustrated*. Willy's long speech (lines 148–180) reveals his pride as a salesman. He also doesn't want his sons to support him financially. The stage directions—"[*desperation is on him now*]" (line 186) and "[*grasping HOWARD'S arm*]" (line 261)—show Willy's desperate reaction to Howard's refusal. Willy's anger reveals his frustration over a no-win situation.

7. Three descriptions that apply to Howard are *insensitive*, *impatient*, and *bored*. Howard is totally insensitive to Willy's emotional and financial needs. Howard also shows no regard for Willy's thirty-four years of service to the firm. The stage directions—"[*barely interested*]" (line 147) and "[*impatiently*]" (line 201)—reveal Howard's boredom and impatience.

GED PRACTICE: DRAMA
pages 222-227

1. (5) **Characterization**
   You can conclude that Eddie's attachment to May is based on jealousy and possessiveness. He threatens to fight her dates and says, "You'll never escape me either. I'll track you down no matter where you go."

2. (1) **Making Inferences**
   A fifteen-year relationship filled with desperation, misunderstanding, and possessiveness is unhealthy.

3. (2) **Characterization**
   The word *now* is italicized three times in May's dialogue (lines 23–25). According to May's remarks, you can infer that his feelings for her are unpredictable.

4. (4) **Stage Directions**
   You can conclude that taking a drink and slamming a bottle reveal her anger.

5. (4) **Application**
   May's immediate problem is how to handle the difficulties in her relationship.

6. (2) **Stage Directions**
   The stage directions state that a *tone of politely feigned interest, masking indifference* (lines 28–30) characterizes Brick's speech with Margaret.

7. (1) **Setting**
   Margaret says she could "utter a scream you could hear across the Arkansas border an' parts of Louisiana an' Tennessee." All these states are located in the South.

8. **(5) Making Inferences**
The children belong to Gooper and Mae. Mae is Brick's sister-in-law (line 76). Therefore, you can assume that Gooper is Brick's brother.

9. **(4) Setting**
In lines 84–85, Margaret refers to Big Daddy's birthday.

10. **(1) Main Idea**
Margaret repeatedly calls the children "no-neck monsters" to describe their appearance. She complains about their screaming and table manners.

11. **(4) Application**
Margaret is the only person onstage in this passage. Brick is in the shower. You hear his voice, but he is "unseen." Since Margaret is the center of attention, the camera would focus on her.

12. **(2) Characterization**
Ruth calls Big Walter "a good man," and Mama agrees, "Yes, a fine man." These statements reveal their respect for him.

13. **(1) Plot**
Mama says that Big Walter "grieved hisself" over their baby's death.

14. **(5) Characterization**
Although Big Walter could be "hard-headed, mean, kind of wild with women," Mama accepted his faults and sympathized with his problems.

15. **(3) Making Inferences**
Mama says in the concluding line of dialogue that Big Walter "just couldn't never catch up with his dreams, that's all."

16. **(2) Stage Directions**
This gesture emphasizes the thoughtfulness of Ruth's response to Mama: "Yes, life can be a barrel of disappointments, sometimes."

17. **(4) Application**
Big Walter once told Mama, "Seem like God didn't see fit to give the black man nothing but dreams—but He did give us children to make them dreams seem worthwhile." Therefore, you can conclude that if Big Walter were still alive, he would agree that children represent the hopes of the future.

CHAPTER 8: COMMENTARIES ON THE ARTS

EXERCISE 1
pages 232-233

Part I

1.		2.		3.		4.	
(1)	F	(1)	F	(1)	O	(1)	F
(2)	F	(2)	F	(2)	O	(2)	F
(3)	O	(3)	O	(3)	O	(3)	O
						(4)	O

Part II

1. 3	2. 4	3. 1	4. 3

EXERCISE 2
pages 235-236

Part I
Your answer should include any four of the following adjectives: electric, great, spectacular, strongest, most energetic.

Part II
Your answer should include any four of the following adjectives: big, brash, strong, mature, tremendous, clear, good.

Part III
Your answer should include any two of the following adjectives: readable, wonderful, best.

Part IV
1. A nuclear power plant releases a radioactive mist that turns some schoolchildren into monsters. The nasty tykes commit such despicable acts as killing their parents with deadly hugs.
2. predictable
3. dreadful

EXERCISE 3
pages 238-239

1. **(4)** The purpose of the passage is to describe the Harlem Unit's original production of the play, which was "no ordinary version of Shakespeare" (lines 5–6).
2. Your summary should include these details: Prompted by witches, Macbeth conspires with his wife and murders the King of Scotland.
3. Scotland
4. Haiti
5. "full of voodoo drums and witches' cries" (lines 21–22)
6. (1) F (4) O
   (2) F (5) F
   (3) O (6) F
7. **(3)** Brooks Atkinson states this opinion in the concluding line of the passage.
8. **(1)** Atkinson's flattering remarks about the play reveal his enthusiasm.

EXERCISE 4
pages 240-241

1. **(2)** The passage presents several examples of humorous dialogue and comic situations in "The Honeymooners."
2. **(3)** The first paragraph details the setting of "The Honeymooners." The Kramdens rented a cheap apartment on Chauncy Street in Brooklyn.
3. **(2)** The dialogue from the script familiarizes the reader with the show's characters and comic situations.
4. **(5)** The excerpt from the TV script (lines 46–54) illustrates a joke about Ralph's weight.

5. (4) By highlighting the funny moments from the show, the authors are trying to show that "The Honeymooners" is an entertaining situation comedy.

EXERCISE 5
pages 242-243

1. (2) The author uses this technique to arouse the reader's curiosity about the film. By watching *The 39 Steps*, the reader would discover the answers to those questions.
2. (5) The concluding sentence states that an ordinary man like Hannay typifies many Hitchcock heroes.
3. The statements should be numbered in this order: 5, 3, 6, 1, 4, 2.
4. (4) The headline describes an average man who apparently finds himself involved in a murder mystery. You can conclude that Hitchcock would find this man's predicament intriguing.
5. (3) The critic states that "this thrilling espionage adventure was the first film to establish Hitchcock as the Master of Suspense" (lines 1–2). There is not enough information to determine whether the critic thinks that *The 39 Steps* was Hitchcock's best work, choice (1).

EXERCISE 6
pages 244-245

1. blue-collar housewives (line 5)
2. (1) The description "pure, strong, soulful voice" (lines 6–7) suggests that Loretta Lynn's singing is powerful and moving.
3. (5) In lines 23–24, the author contrasts the two singers' messages: "While Tammy Wynette, ever the romanticist, was singing 'Stand By Your Man,' Loretta was saying 'stand up to your man.'"
4. (4) The song titles "Don't Come Home A-Drinkin'" and "You Ain't Woman Enough To Take My Man" were aimed directly at her husband, Mooney. These two examples illustrate that Loretta Lynn's songs are about personal relationships and experiences.
5. (2) Loretta Lynn's quotation states, "We have just as much right to get some fun out of life as they [men] do" (lines 22–23).

EXERCISE 7
pages 246-247

1. They taught themselves.
2. Harlem
3. (4) Nick Castle, a choreographer, "designed many of the Nicholas Brothers' routines." Therefore, you can infer that a choreographer's job is to create or design dances.
4. (2) Throughout the passage, the author directly quotes Nicholas's comments about the development of his tap-dancing career.

5. (1) Leapfrogging down a staircase and landing in full splits are acrobatic moves.

EXERCISE 8
pages 248-249

1. "The Rickety Wheel Makes the Most Noise"
2. comic, serious, dreamlike
3. Chile
4. (5) Laura Montenegro states in paragraph 4: "What we'd like to accomplish is to make people get a little more insight into our humanness."
5. (4) You can infer from the author's favorable description of the Montenegros' creative ideas that he respects both the artists and their work.
6. (1) I   **(2)** V   **(3)** V   **(4)** I   **(5)** I

EXERCISE 9
pages 250-251

1. The sculpture shows the influence of her Indian heritage. Edmonia Lewis's mother belonged to the Chippewa tribe.
2. (1) to learn marble-carving techniques
(2) to pursue her career with greater artistic freedom
(3) to avoid racial discrimination
3. (2) The author states that Indians are often characterized as "brutal and savage."
4. (3) The passage states that the sculpture shows "a moment of quiet reflection being enjoyed by father and daughter." The reviewer says the small size of the sculpture expresses the intimacy of the moment.

EXERCISE 10
pages 252-253

1. (3) The introductory sentence states, "Tattoo artists have always felt that their work deserved more acceptance as an art." A museum exhibit of tattoo art replicas would be a form of recognition.
2. (3) The supporting details in the second paragraph summarize the ancient historical background of tattoo art. The authors specify dates and locations.
3. (5) The authors state in lines 3–4, "It is easy to see the craft, the fancy, the individuality, and the art of the practitioner." Therefore, you can conclude that the authors appreciate the artistic qualities of tattooing.
4. (1) I   **(2)** V   **(3)** I   **(4)** I

EXERCISE 11
pages 254-255

1. (5) The passage discusses mainly the character of the fictional detective.
2. (2) Lines 5–6 state that the hard-boiled detective "was born in America."

3. (2) Lines 17–18 state that the origins of the detective were in the lonesome pioneer.

4. (3) Chandler states in lines 39–40 that the fictional American detective is "a relatively poor man."

5. (4) Line 33 states that Philip Marlowe used similes. In the chapter on poetry, you learned that similes, a type of figurative language, are direct comparisons using the words *as* or *like*.

EXERCISE 12
pages 256-257

1. (2) Paragraph 1 states, "No other writer is asked to commit words to paper with such speed, under such pressure." Therefore, you can conclude that the journalist, unlike the novelist or the poet, is pressured to meet strict deadlines.

2. (3) Both Leo Tolstoy and John Ciardi restate the importance of the writing rule "Show, don't tell."

3. (1) (b)—This sentence specifically states the umpire's decision and shows you the coach's angry gestures.

　　(2) (a)—The verb *arrested* conveys a stronger action than *took into custody. Unregistered handgun* is a more precise image than *illegal weapon. Mayor* is more specific than *man.*

　　(3) (b)—The sentence shows you how the woman developed her skills and specifies both the woman's original position and her new position.

EXERCISE 13
pages 258-259

1. (1) F　　**(3)** O　　**(5)** O　　**(7)** F
　　(2) F　　**(4)** O　　**(6)** F　　**(8)** O

2. She melts the witch with a bucket of cleaning water.

3. (5) The author uses the introductory sentence of many fairy tales to begin the book review because he is writing about *The Wonderful Wizard of Oz.*

4. (3) Paragraph 2 states the major theme: "The power of Good is greater than the power of Evil."

GED PRACTICE: COMMENTARIES ON THE ARTS
pages 260-265

1. (3) Supporting Details
A building designed in the shape of a turtle is unique. The other choices describe the center's less remarkable characteristics.

2. (2) Identifying Opinions
Lines 19–21 state that Dennis Sun Rhodes believed "it was important that modern architecture be adapted to traditional Indian values."

3. (4) Main Idea
The second paragraph describes the building's size, rooms, and spatial arrangement.

4. (1) Style and Structure
Because the author's purpose is to instruct the reader, the tone is informative.

5. (1) Application
Like the Indian Center, churches also show the influence of meaningful cultural symbols. For example, stained glass windows of biblical scenes, statues of religious figures, and the cross are symbols of Christianity.

6. (3) Supporting Details
The fifth paragraph states that in a Gallup Poll, TV ran neck-and-neck with unemployment as a major family problem.

7. (4) Making Inferences
The author shows how families who watch a lot of television are not actively participating with each other.

8. (3) Figurative Language
While the husband is completely absorbed watching sports events on television, he's not paying any attention to his wife. Therefore, she is being ignored.

9. (5) Making Inferences
The author voices her concerns about family communication in the final paragraph of the excerpt.

10. (5) Application
The author is concerned that "when you are watching, you aren't doing," so she would probably advise families to participate in actually *doing* things together.

11. (5) Distinguishing Facts from Opinions
This statement interprets how Emily Dickinson's view of the world is reflected in her poems.

12. (2) Supporting Details
Lines 16–17 state, "She seems to have been, more than other poets, writing just for herself."

13. (2) Main Idea
The entire paragraph details the way in which Emily Dickinson observed nature, people, and herself.

4. (4) Supporting Details
You know from the excerpt that Emily Dickinson wrote about death. However, there is not sufficient evidence to support that those poems reflected a morbid fear of death.

15. (3) Making Inferences
Lines 1–4 state that Emily Dickinson "lived a very secluded life. She was alone most of the time; she didn't know other writers."
Therefore, you can infer that she was a solitary person.

16. (5) Application
You know from the passage that Emily Dickinson lived in the nineteenth century; therefore, she could not have written about jukeboxes, which hadn't been invented yet.

Index